EVERYTHING HAS MEANING

WHAT THE TREE STAND MURDERS TAUGHT ME ABOUT LIFE, DEATH, AND DESTINY

SCOTT ROUX

ZAMIZ PRESS

BIOGRAPHY & AUTOBIOGRAPHY / Personal Memoirs

BIOGRAPHY & AUTOBIOGRAPHY / Native Americans

Special discounts are available on quantity purchases by corporations, associations and others. For details, contact the author.

DO YOU HAVE A MESSAGE TO SHARE WITH THE WORLD? ARE YOU INTERESTED IN HAVING YOUR BOOK PUBLISHED? VISIT ZAMIZPRESS.COM

Cover design by Nathaniel Dasco

Everything has Meaning: What the Tree Stand Murders Taught me About Life, Death, and Destiny — 1st Edition

ISBN: 978-1-949813-21-0 and 978-1-949813-25-8

CONTENTS

I dedicate this book to my father and best friend, Dennis Roux. My wings took me into the unknown. With your wisdom and guidance, I traveled the Circle of Life. I dedicate this book to the memory of those lost in the Blue Hills near Rice Lake, Wisconsin on November 21, 2004.

PREFACE

THE THREE GREATEST MYSTERIES IN LIFE are who am I, why am I here, and what is life all about? If you could solve one, you might be the most sought-after person in the world. More importantly, you would possess knowledge that may change everything for you.

What if I told you not one person or experience in our life—good or bad—is random or unintended? If that's true we should be able to look back on our journey. Each person and experience would hold a clue to help us solve life's mysteries. I wonder if we would know what to look for? If not, would it all be lost forever?

I have had some successes and failures. I have hopes and fears. I have lived through terrible tragedies and suffered great losses. I have also done the impossible and witnessed miracles.

For a good part of my sixty-year journey I have felt alone,

uninformed, and at a disadvantage. Yes, there were times I felt blessed and even a little bit lucky. Most of the time I felt like life just happened to me, until something happened. It all started on one summer day in 1992.

It lasted only a few minutes. But it was long enough for me to know it was intentional. When it was over, I felt different. Something changed deep inside me. I felt chosen. I did not know what any of it meant for a very long time. I had to have answers. On that summer day I knew I would not stop until I figured this out.

Later, I realized my experience connected to everything in my life—everything before and everything that came after. It was a new beginning for me. The rest of my life would be different. That day I reached a turning point. It was the beginning of my awakening. I would never be alone or unsure again.

1

IT BEGINS WITH MURDER

> The fear of death follows from the fear of life. A man who lives fully is prepared to die at any time. —**Mark Twain**

November 21, 2004—Blue Hills east of Rice Lake, Wisconsin

It was the Sunday before Thanksgiving. At one o'clock in the afternoon the phone rang in Minnetrista, Minnesota. It was my father, Dennis Roux.

Every year about 650,000 avid, licensed deer hunters flowed into the woodlands all over Wisconsin to bag a deer. These true hunters are dedicated outdoorsmen. They celebrate the rich traditions of the hunting season across our state. I thought maybe Dad was calling to tell me he bagged his deer already. Although it was still early on opening day, I knew Dad had hunted those woods more times than I could count. Maybe he'd had some good luck this year.

Dad went hunting with one of our distant cousins. My brother, and I were busy with other things, but we knew Dad would have fun without us. He would rejoin most of the hunting buddies he had hunted with for decades.

They had asked me to go hunting three times that year. Dad asked me once and my distant cousin asked twice. Each time I said I had other plans. My reasons, in 2004, were a lot of things. My wife had lost her job. Money was tight. It was a busy time with Conwood. And, I had a poker tournament at the house. I was busy. I did not want to go deer hunting this time. I went the year before with my stepbrother. It was enough for a while. I'm just not into deer hunting as much as others in the family. I had other plans in 2004.

Dad asked if I had seen the news. I told him I had not. There was a long silence.

I could tell he was not himself. I thought I heard him breaking down. He was crying quietly. He tried to keep control of his emotions and forced out the words. A lot of people got shot today. A man went crazy. Shot a lot of them. The man had trespassed on private property. Some people were dead, and others were on the way to the hospital. My distant cousin was shot in the stomach, and he was on his way to the hospital.

I was in shock. I think I asked Dad if he was all right, and if I should come up to help. He said not to come. Then he was unable to talk except to tell me he would call later. After we hung up, I just stood there alone in the house. I realized he could have been shot and he could have died. That's when I called my wife.

Between the TV news and my step-mother, Francine, I learned about the shooter. He was a hunter who sneaked onto private property and was found in someone's tree stand. Cross words were exchanged between the property owner and the trespasser. News media said the shooter lost his temper and went on a rampage shooting people. In the end, he had shot eight in my dad's hunting party. Six of them died.

I learned from Francine that during the rampage shooting in the woods, most hunters in Dad's party were still in the cabin area. Some had gotten back from hunting and some others had not gone hunting yet. Some were eating breakfast. Some were getting ready to go out. As the gunfire popped in the woods like firecrackers, one of my distant cousins told my dad there was family out there who might need help. He had a pickup truck and asked Dad to go with him into the shooting zone.

Several hunters there said Dad did not hesitate. Without a word and without his gun, Dad jumped into the back of the pickup truck and left the safety of the cabin area. They drove into the woods and the line of fire. At that time no one knew who or where the shooter or shooters were, and they did not know their intentions. Police and emergency services had not yet come onto the scene. After a long while, my cousin and father returned with two seriously injured hunters in the bed of the truck. Dad was attending to them. Denny was in bad condition. Dad applied pressure to the gunshot wound in his stomach.

Looking back, I know Dad was unable to talk on the phone because he had just returned from hell. I can see him now with blood on his hands and clothes, holding the phone to his head, his eyes staring into space. Dad would have been standing in the middle of the chaos—ambulances and police cars racing around, the wounded and dead being moved on stretchers, the police frantically searching for the shooter or shooters, helicopters flying overhead like a MASH unit and media descending on them with cameras and sound booms. When I talked to my dad on the phone that first afternoon, he didn't tell me what he had done. Even weeks later he did not talk about the details of his time in the woods during the rescue mission.

There has been a lot reported and much written about the shooting in the Blue Hills east of Rice Lake. Ten years later a book came out—*The Tree Stand Murders* by David Whitehurst. The book told the story of the shooter, his troubled life, the conflict on private property, the shooting rampage, and the tragic ending. Whitehurst followed the criminal trial. A jury convicted Chai Soua Vang on six counts of first-degree murder and three counts of attempted murder. Mr. Whitehurst wrote about the trial and the sentencing of Mr. Vang. He got life in prison for each of the six murder convictions. The book shows it was even more chilling than I could have imagined—the six dead hunters were unarmed and four of the six were shot in the back.

Out of respect for the victims and families I will not rehash details of the event. I devote parts of this book to the tragedy and aftermath from the view of my father and myself. The impact on our family has been and continues to be significant. 106 days later, my father died. Like many others close to this nightmare, I believe the stress, fear, pain, and unsettled feelings were carried from that day and contributed to deaths. We can never forget the men and women with invisible wounds.

Tragic events like the Deer Stand Murders triggered many things—new gun laws, more gun-safety regulations, more rules for hunters, changes in private property postings, hunting etiquette, and in-the-field dispute resolution protocol. These get the attention of the public. But there are other things this tragedy triggered—things as important but not talked about enough.

For me, this horrific tragedy opened my eyes, in new ways. I believe we each collect life experiences that teach us how to live. Our collection is what defines who we are and how we live. Some of the interpretations of our collected experiences are accurate and good. Others are inaccurate, untrue, and can hold us back. Regardless, each of these interpretations becomes a part of our judgment and behavior process. It is how we make decisions in life, how we act. We use our unique interpretations of life's experiences as our guide. We carry them deep inside, where we are all alone.

When my father risked his life to give others a chance to live, his heroism validated one of the most important beliefs in my life, that my father was a hero! I wanted to be like him. The awful events of November 21, 2004, and my father's heroic actions, validated my thoughts.

That unexpected validation had benefits. It gave me

confidence in my ability to see and feel truth in the world, on my own. Dad's actions gave me a strength I had not known before. I would no longer wander through life. I would live more self-assured.

After that tragic day, I started to reevaluate my life. This time the important things seemed to jump out at me. I realized my steadily increasing and moving eagle encounters were more important than I had thought. I realized my vivid dreams were telling me things. The signs and symbols lighting up my bedroom walls meant something more than I thought. I realized my chilling birth and my Chippewa Indian roots mattered. I realized the native Indian heritage flowing through my veins, and my given Chippewa name defined me. Nothing is random. After the deer hunting tragedy and my father's actions, my eyes were opened. Everything has meaning.

2

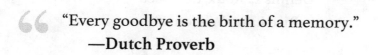

"Every goodbye is the birth of a memory."
—Dutch Proverb

December 21, 2006—Pittsburgh, Pennsylvania

My father's actions on November 21, 2004, did have an enormous impact on me, but there is more to the story. There were others that committed extraordinary acts of heroism that day. Two years later, on December 21, 2006, the Carnegie Hero Fund Commission recognized these heroes along with others across the country who had risked their lives to an extraordinary degree while saving or attempting to save the lives of others. My family was proud to see my father's name on the honored list of heroes from the deer-stand tragedy.

Lauren D. Hesebeck
Rice Lake, Wisconsin

Carter L. Crotteau
Haugen, Wisconsin

Jessica M. Willers, deceased
Green Bay, Wisconsin

Allan James Laski, deceased
Haugen, Wisconsin

Dennis L. Roux, deceased
Rice Lake, Wisconsin

The Carnegie Hero Fund Commission Award has existed for more than a century. Andrew Carnegie, the renowned industrialist-philanthropist, established the fund to recognize heroes for their acts of courage and in some cases their sacrifices. Since the start of the fund more than 9,000 heroes have been recognized in the United States and Canada. In addition to the honor, each recipient receives a grant of $5,000. Since its inception, the Carnegie Hero Fund has distributed over $29,000,000 in the form of grants, death benefits, scholarships, and financial assistance. Below is the posting by the Carnegie Fund recognizing the deer stand heroes:

On November 21, 2004, near Birchwood, Wisconsin,
Terry S. Willers, 47, was deer hunting on private
property with several others, including Dennis R.
Drew, 55, and Lauren D. Hesebeck, 48, automobile
sales manager. They and other members of the party
confronted a trespasser on the property and directed
him to leave. The trespasser, armed with a rifle,
started to walk away but then opened fire on the
hunters, wounding Willers, Drew and Hesebeck, and
killing three others. Although a vehicle nearby was
available to him, Hesebeck remained at the scene to
tend Willers and Drew. At the party's nearby cabin,
Carter L. Crotteau, 18, college student, who was the
son and brother of two of the hunters who were
killed, was alerted by radio to the shooting and,
despite not knowing the assailant's whereabouts,
responded by all-terrain vehicle with Willers's son.
They evacuated Willers from the scene, Hesebeck
again electing to remain, with Drew. Hearing her
father's voice on a radio transmission, Jessica M.
Willers, 27, surgical technician, and Allan James
Laski, 43, lumber yard manager, also members of the
hunting party, set out to the scene from the cabin on
all-terrain vehicle. En route, they too were shot and
mortally wounded by the assailant. The assailant
reappeared at the point near Hesebeck and saw that
he was alive. He fired again at Hesebeck, then fled.
Two other members of the hunting party, Dennis L.

Roux, 63, retired union officer, and Drew's brother, arrived in a pickup truck and took Hesebeck and Drew to safety. Roux tending Drew in the truck's bed. Willers required hospital treatment for his wound, and he recovered. Drew, also hospitalized, died the next day of his injury. Hesebeck was hospitalized for treatment, including surgery of a shoulder wound and recovered.

My daughter, Kaitlyn, had a wonderful relationship with Grandpa Dennis Roux. I always saw my dad as a man of character, and I knew Kaitlyn and my son, Ryan, did too. But Kaitlyn also saw my dad as goofy and funny. I think that is a powerful memory for her to hold onto. Although Kaitlyn was young in Grandpa's days, she does remember the sleepovers at the house at Rice Lake. And she remembers one of the rules; the kids had to wake up Grandpa before they could go outside. I know he wanted to watch over them, but I also think he wanted to be with them. They would catch sunfish and bluegills in the pond, and we would have a fish fry, in the summertime. We also would eat a lot of German dishes passed down through the family and enjoyed at holidays. Kaitlyn was appointed the official taster by my dad. That way she got to eat more than the others. Even in the winter, the kids loved visiting. They ice fished together. They would cut a hole in the ice and patiently wait. We often saw deer, an occasional eagle and owl, and every once in a while, a bear. Those childhood memories we all have with my dad and

Frannie are all good. They helped shape character and love of family.

After the Deer Stand Murders, Frannie said my father acted different. He did not want to go outside as much or leave the house. And he did not like being alone.

He was exposed to the shooter, and at that time he had no idea where the shooter was or what his intentions were. Regardless, Dad stayed with my cousin the whole time, pressing on the wound for five miles. All the way out of the woods and up to the bait shop where they met the ambulances.

They took my cousin from the bait shop to Marshfield Hospital nine miles away. We lost my cousin the next day. He never recovered from his terrible wound. That tragic outcome and all the pain and losses of those days shook my dad to his core. As I said before, he died 106 days later. I believe his medical problems were a factor, but the deer-stand shootings ate at his heart and soul. I know it took him from us. After the shooting, Dad suffered from depression, paranoia, and PTSD like many others who lived through those unthinkable moments. As a matter of fact, several died within months of the shootings. Like other major tragedies—9/11 comes to mind —people far away from the actual tragedy suffer tremendous emotional pain and die within months of the event. I believe many hunters and their family members left the woods on November 21, 2004, emotionally wounded. For some, their emotional wounds were fatal. Others who survived that day will never hunt again. Many took that terrible experience and transformed it into a positive outcome. For some it reminded them how important and short and unpredictable life can be. Some renewed old friendships. Some changed their life priorities. And some, like me, learned more about themselves. Their eyes were opened so they could better understand and appreciate their own life journey.

3

> "To witness the birth of a child is our best opportunity to experience the meaning of the word miracle." —Thomas Wolfe

September 13, 1961—Deaconess Hospital—Milwaukee, Wisconsin

They gave my mom and me last rites before I was born! All good Catholics know last rites are the final prayers given to people of faith shortly before their death. Well, since we are both here, I guess you could say we dodged a major bullet! The story I was told, since I was a baby at the time, was that my dad, Dennis, fell in love with my mom, Neola, in 1960. I came along on September 13, 1961—Scott Douglas Anthony Roux. Grandma Kathleen Roux (my rock as long as she walked on this earth) told me I was a miracle baby. I remember how good that made me feel. I was five. But I don't remember why it came up; whether I asked her or if she just said it one day. I remember it made me feel very special and that was good. When I was a kid, I needed to feel loved, some praise and encouragement because often I didn't feel so good. I struggled in a lot of ways as a kid. I remember Grandma Kathleen watched out for me. She told me a lot of things at the kitchen table on West Van Beck in Milwaukee.

My Mom, Neola, was a small person and I was a big baby. To add to the birthing problem, Neola carried me into the tenth month—September. I read in a normal, nine-month pregnancy a baby can add one pound a week in the last month. So, I got bigger every day and Neola got deeper into a problem. Deaconess Hospital came into the picture. There can be all sorts of complications with a pregnancy, especially the first one. No experience is a problem because you don't know the difference between normal and a problem.

I think for my mother each change probably seemed minor. Another new ache or pain. Water retention. Cravings and mood swings. The trouble is babies roll around a lot inside a mother's belly. Sometimes that can cause some trouble. Pregnancy problems can get serious if they're not attended to by a doctor. For example, a routine infection can become dangerous if it's not treated early. All I know is my mother had trouble because she was small and I was big, and there were other complications. Because I was too big to be born the normal way, we were taken to Deaconess Hospital where a specialist did an emergency cesarean section. We were given our last rites first. It did not look good for us. C-sections can have serious complications. The baby can suffocate, and the mother can bleed to death.

I am happy to report everything came out okay. Looking back with the eyes of a man, my birth experience was the first thing to happen to me completely out of my control. I could have been over before I started! And my near-death birth would not be the last time I overcame some very dangerous moments in my life. My near-death birth experience and the other cliffhanging moments in my life had no special meaning to me for a very long time. After the November 21, 2004, experience I opened my eyes and looked at everything differently. I began to understand that for me to get where I am today, everything had to happen exactly as it did. If any one of my life experiences had a different outcome, I would not be who I am today. That reality came into focus after the Deer Stand Shootings and again after my father's premature death. Those events in my life made me realize everything happens for a reason. Therefore, we must embrace each experience and what message is being sent. What am I supposed to realize? I know I am here for a reason. It is my sole responsibility to seek the answers and grow.

If I had died at birth, I would not have Kaitlyn and Ryan. I would not know Grandma Kathleen and Grandpa Larry or Dad or my stepmom, Francine. I would not have had my brother, Greg, and my step-brother, Jeff, and half-sister, Sherry. If I had not been born to Dennis and Neola, I would not have my Chippewa blood. I would not have my Indian name—White Thunderbird, Eagle! I would not have experienced and understood the eagles visiting me and the vivid dreams and the symbols and signs that light up my bedroom walls. As I review my life experiences it is clear to me that everything has meaning. I was supposed to survive birth. My birth mother was supposed to be Neola and she was supposed to put Greg in my life, too—he was born on the same exact day as me, September 13, two years later.

I believe we must pay very close attention to our life experiences. We must seek to understand. And we must trust our interpretation of reality in this world.

4

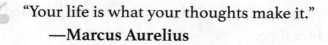

"Your life is what your thoughts make it."
—Marcus Aurelius

March 7, 2021—Boulder City, Nevada

My daughter's girlfriends at the University of Minnesota decided to go to Texas on spring break 2021. Naturally, Kaitlyn wanted to go. Naturally, I said no. She was a freshman. In a father's protective mind, she was not ready for an unchaperoned road trip with a group of college girls looking for fun. I think most parents would agree—there are just too many things that can go wrong. To add to it, money was tight. The high cost of college is no secret. It is a big financial challenge for most people. Even with help from a partial scholarship and part-time work, the financial burden can be unbearable at times. When I'm pushing my Kaitlyn to keep her grades up to hold onto her scholarship, and I'm pushing her to find a part-time job, it made no sense to add the financial burden of a midterm Texas vacation with additional costs for gas, room and board, and entertainment! She can do that out of her own pocket someday. Right then, it was coming out of my pocket and therefore was not in the cards.

Instead of the all-expenses-paid Texas extravaganza, I suggested she visit me in Boulder City, Nevada. I sold our house in Rice Lake, Wisconsin, a year earlier—another story for later— and a visit during spring break would be good for both of us. Because she warmed up to the idea so fast, I figured she was not all that into the Texas road trip. I'd like to think Kaitlyn needed some dad time as much as I needed some daughter time.

Soon after her arrival, we looked for some things to do together. That's when we planned the day trip to the Grand Canyon. The West Canyon, part of the 277-mile-long Grand Canyon, was just a few hours away. At the time, I never considered the possibility something special could happen that would transform our little trip into an unforgettable father-daughter moment. Even the breathtaking immensity of the Grand Canyon would pale in comparison to what happened to us. I understood immediately. I knew what it meant. Now Kaitlyn would know what it meant. It would no longer be one of Dad's stories or theories. When it happened, I knew we were exactly where we were supposed to be on the seventh day in March 2021, coincidentally the same day my father passed.

Before I go there, I must line up the key pieces that led to this unforgettable event. It begins with the fact that I always have to stay busy. I never sit still. I remember the good times as a kid in Milwaukee, living with Grandma Kathleen and Grandpa Larry on West Van Beck. The summers were great. Every morning after my paper route, I went across the street to Wilson Park, to their olympic pool, and swam alone. I swam laps until I dropped. Then, I played sports the rest of the day until I dropped—baseball, football, and basketball. When I wasn't doing sports, I was looking for paying work; yards to mow, leaves to rake, hedges to trim. Anything to stay busy and make money. In the winter, I shoveled snow. I also found time to play ice hockey and go tobogganing and trade baseball cards.

Later, as a teen, I stayed busy working on cars or at one of my many jobs after school. Then, I stayed busy in the Army, Navy, and college in California. I worked three jobs and paid my own way. All that to say staying busy is a major trait, and I passed it onto my daughter. Like me, Kaitlyn must always stay busy. She got my stay-busy gene for sure. I am sure our rapidly organized Grand Canyon day trip happened because we are both so alike. Looking back, I am sure everything happened as it did for a reason.

That morning we got into the car, put in some Johnny Cash and Waylon Jennings CDs, and headed for one of the seven wonders of the world. We talked about a lot of things on the way there. We learned the Colorado River carved out the Grand Canyon seventeen million years ago. The 277 miles long canyon is up to eighteen miles wide and a mile deep in places. As we talked about it, we got even more excited about our newest adventure. I could not have prepared for what we were about to see. No picture could do it justice.

I was so wrapped up in the Grand Canyon that I did not think about my eagles. They have been following me for decades. On this trip, I did not think about what could happen, although I did know the bald eagle is one of the 350 species of birds that inhabit the region.

By 2021, the Roux family and my closest friends knew about my eagle encounters. They are many, and they are meaningful to me. Especially after the Deer Stand Murders and the death of my father a few months later. I know my eagle encounters (we will talk about later) are much more than random events. They are more significant than just a big bird flying overhead. As I have learned over my life, there will always be people who do not see, understand, or appreciate the spiritual aspects of life. That is okay. It is for each of us to work out on our own. I believe when one approaches events and people (that enter their life) with an open mind and a pure heart, the real answers eventually come. Albert Einstein said there are two ways to live life. One is as though nothing is a miracle. The other is as though everything is a miracle. I choose the latter. And I understand and respect those who choose the former.

Our drive was a few hours long. Kaitlyn and I parked the car at Eagle Point in Arizona, on the edge of Grand Canyon West. The special attraction at that location is the Skywalk, a seventy-foot-long horseshoe-shaped glass walkway that projects out over the canyon. It is 3,500 feet above the

Colorado River and is designed to withstand an 8.0 magnitude earthquake within fifty miles. We joined one of the tours that took us on the Skywalk and into a Native American Village with various dwellings: the Hualapai, Hopi, Navajo, and Havasupai Indians. We enjoyed our time just taking in the spectacular views from the edge of the Grand Canyon and listening to the tour guide talk about the rich history of the area.

I never realized there were so many ways to explore the Grand Canyon: jeep, van, bus, horseback, bike, hiking, helicopter, train, airplane, skydiving, camping, and rafting. This time we were happy to just walk around Eagle Point and listen to the tour guide. Along the way we met a Navajo Elder. He was an interesting man. He explained to me the eagle shadow that appears on the canyon wall as the sun sets. I thought being at Eagle Point, and with my eagle-encounter history, we would see one for sure. Instead, as we went on our tour that day the skies were empty. There were no eagles in the area.

The Navajo Elder told me the bald eagle was not native to the Grand Canyon. Not until after the construction of the Glen Canyon Dam in 1963 did the bald eagle appear in the region. They started to spend winters in the canyon in 1985. The Elder said the eagles fished the clear waters. He said they are most often seen in the Nankoweap Creek area where the trout spawn. Unfortunately, that area is more than a hundred miles from Eagle Point, Arizona. Still, they saw their fair share of eagles there. Just not as often or lately.

That day, Kaitlyn and I enjoyed our time together. We

enjoyed the spectacular Grand Canyon experience and the Navajo Elder. Because Neola, my biological mother, is 50 percent Chippewa Indian and I am 16 percent Chippewa I got very involved in learning about my Indian heritage- Mole Lake Ojibwe. A good portion of my journey revealed in this book draws upon my Chippewa roots. Kaitlyn has the last of the Chippewa blood flowing through her veins, and she is proud of her genetic heritage. I lovingly tease her—she's the last of the Mohicans. At the end, the tour group broke up and tourists returned to their buses. Kaitlyn and I hung out. We took our time standing on the edge of the canyon alone just taking in the beauty of the world. Then it happened.

Out of nowhere the eagles came! They were not tiny dots a mile away deep in the canyon. They were close and they were big. Somewhat in surprise, we just stood there and watched the two big bald eagles come right to us on a straight line. It was as if they were looking right at us and were on their way for a reason.

We watched as they approached. Once they got close, they soared upward and then circled above, their heads looking down at where we stood. The feeling of connection was intense. Like most Native Americans, the Chippewa believe the eagle is a messenger delivering messages to and from the Great Spirit. An eagle sighting can be delivery of a message or an affirmation that your prayers have been heard or you are protected. We were alone, just me, Kaitlyn, and the two majestic eagles circling above us. I have come to believe my eagle encounters are very special because to the Chippewa Indians they represent strength and power. They are the chief among the winged creatures. For me, the eagle is a spirit animal and powerful messenger from God.

That day, as the eagles finished circling overhead before turning from us to ride the winds into the heart of the Grand Canyon, we stood quietly and respectfully. We reveled in the command performance. I was happy our day together at the Grand Canyon ended that way. We will never forget. I believe they waited for the perfect moment.

5

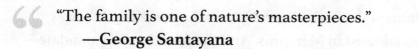

> "The family is one of nature's masterpieces."
> —**George Santayana**

> "A loving heart is the truest wisdom."
> —**Charles Dickens**

Milwaukee, Wisconsin—1966 and more

Like a lot of young marriages in the 1960s, Neola and Dennis split up after five years and went their separate ways. I was five and my brother, Greg, three. My dad took us with him. We moved in with Grandma Kathleen and Grandpa Larry on West Van Beck Avenue.

Today, I can appreciate how difficult life had to be for blue-collar workers back in the sixties in large industrial cities like Milwaukee. The workers were dealing with a lot of blood, sweat, and tears from long hours, long workweeks, and demanding physical jobs. In the sixties, they faced things like unions, strikes, wage and price freezes, foreign competition, downsizing, layoffs, and long periods of unemployment. It did not help that most of the American population at the time was youthful—over seventy million baby boomers had moved into adulthood and entered the workforce. It was a lot of people with little work or life experience. Most were just getting married young and starting families. They quickly got into debt up to their ears.

The 1960s were difficult for most Americans everywhere. The President of the United States—John F Kennedy—was assassinated in Dallas. The noted Baptist minister and Civil Rights activist—Reverend Martin Luther King, Jr.—was assassinated in Memphis. And the presidential candidate— Robert F. Kennedy—was assassinated in Los Angeles. To add to the tragedies, the unpopular Vietnam War fueled student marches on college campuses across the country. The Helter-Skelter Manson Family killing spree put people on edge. And the Watts Riots in Los Angeles stirred up racial unrest and fueled civil rights marches across the South.

I believe the older generation got stirred up because everything in their world seemed to be changing before their eyes. The Beatles came over from England and changed all the music, and rock & roll and Elvis Presley were blasphemies in the Bible Belt. The sixties were a time when people experimented with sex and drugs. Those who fought the World Wars to guarantee America freedom were in shock. They believed their world was falling apart, when, in fact, it was coming together bigger and better. I believe the clashes were not a fight to stop equal rights. I believe it was fear of change. Change scares most people.

Dennis and Neola were young and in love in the middle of all the sixties chaos. Like many back then, their marriage was not strong enough to hold together. As a divorced man myself, I understand marriage can be difficult even when both partners have the best of intentions. It is possible to have a good life together with wonderful children and still have some things not work. Parting ways can be the only solution. It is important to search for happiness and meaning. It is not always possible to be all things to somebody, and that's okay. The world does change, and so do we. Maturity is when you can embrace reality and respect others' rights to move at their own pace. When I look back at Neola's and Dennis's divorce, I get it. Thing is, when I was a kid, I did not get it. All I know is I wanted a mother.

My dad was one of five siblings. After his marriage split, we moved in with Dad's mom and dad. It did not register at the time because I was five—but I saw Dad's parents only as my grandparents. Fact was, in 1966, they were in their forties still working and raising their kids: Daniel, Jackie, Rochelle, Paulette, and Dennis the oldest. Looking back, I am in awe of Grandma Kathleen and Grandpa Larry for not hesitating to make room for three more people in their little house on West Van Beck... and my brother, Greg, was still a toddler.

At the time, only two of Dad's siblings were still living at home. And I still think taking us under their roof was a very big deal. The Roux family is strong. Family was the glue that held us together in the good times and the bad. Grandma and Grandpa never made me feel unwanted or that we were in the way. I am so glad because I did not need to add more emotional baggage to my already heavy load. I was a five-year-old kid trying to figure out life.

Grandma Kathleen was and will always be my rock! I love her so much. She watched over me. Grandma Kathleen was like Edith Bunker on the TV show, *All in the Family*. She always wore a dress and her apron and glasses. And she was always busy in the kitchen. She took tender loving care of everyone under her roof. This good Catholic lady made sure we were good Catholic boys! She made us say our prayers every day and go to church on Sunday. I remember spending a lot of time at St. Romans. Seemed to me they had something religious going on all the time: the Epiphany, Ash Wednesday, Palm Sunday, Easter, All Saints' Day, the Feast of the Immaculate Conception, and Christmas... and that's not all of 'em.

She quit school in the eighth grade to work on the family farm. Grandma Kathleen did a lot of things, but one of the most important was she became a skilled baker and taught herself the accordion. When Grandma put her mind to something, it happened. She taught me about *all in*, a behavior trait I lived by all my life. Nothing is worth a halfway effort. Either go all in or find something else. The range of Grandma's accomplishments demonstrates how special she was as a person. Everyone loved her. They were lucky to know her.

I remember wanting a mom so bad that Grandma

Kathleen showed me the way. She had me pray for a mom at least once a week at the kitchen table—just me and her. She told me God hears and sees everything.

She said, "Don't think for a minute that God's not looking for a mom for you. He's looking for the best mom."

I believed everything Grandma said to me. I know she was not perfect. None of us are. But I think she was really close to it.

I got harassed at school because I didn't have a mother! Seems bizarre looking back. How could something like that even happen? It is ridiculous to any developed person. What kind of person would make fun of a person because they did not have a parent? A stupid kid!

I've learned over life kids can do some pretty nasty and stupid things. When you are a kid, you don't see how ridiculous some of these things are. It hurts. You want to avoid it, make it stop. I know I felt inferior to people with mothers. In my kid head I wondered what was wrong with me. My confidence was shattered. I felt like I did not measure up.

It bothered me so much that I ran away when I was eight years old. I did not want to be in that school anymore. I did not want to face the people making fun of me. I was ashamed and embarrassed because my life was different. When the police found me, Grandma Kathleen did not get mad. She held me and helped me. She told me God was looking for a special mother for a special little boy. She said I needed to trust him and be patient. I guess the most important thing I learned from Grandma Kathleen was to believe in something bigger than me. For her, it was God. She said it could be God for me, too. The bigger the better. She said it is the only way you can grow. She said life is bigger than anything or anyone. It is the key to a happy and full life.

Grandpa Larry was a good man, too. He worked for Harley Davidson Motorcycles until he got laid off. Then he worked at the Phillip Orth Company. They milled and traded flour, feed, and grains. They sold bakery supplies as well. Grandpa Larry would bring some baking supplies home, and Grandma Kathleen would bake up a storm. She was an incredible baker. I used to say Grandma's baking was how I got my friends.

Grandpa Larry was different from Grandma Kathleen. He was a man of few words, very regimented, and very strict. He got up in the morning and ate his poached egg, drank his coffee, read his newspaper, watched his morning news, and went to work. When he got home the house got quiet. Greg and I could not go out after dinner to play until Grandpa Larry had finished his dinner, watched his nightly news, and read his evening paper. Then we had to be back inside the house when the first lightning bug flickered. But, in spite of all that, I know Grandpa cared about us in his way. A famous poet once said you don't have to deserve your mother's love. You have to deserve your father's. I think that goes for grandmothers and grandfathers, too.

Grandpa Larry went overboard on the rigidness and the discipline. I think he believed bad behavior only led to more bad behavior, so he couldn't tolerate it. As a father, I can see how kids can wear out a person. But I also know kids do goofy things and make a lot of bad decisions and mistakes. As a father, I also know it does not mean they are on their way to the penitentiary or an early grave! When you are a kid, you are learning. It's the time to try things and screw up. You can't learn without making mistakes and doing stupid things. Parents should not ignore bad behavior. They also don't need to be angry at their children all the time.

One thing I will always be grateful for is that we ate good on our days on West Van Beck: bratwurst, cheese bread, brat-fries, sauerkraut, battered and fried cheese curds, venison, cakes, croissants, danish pastries, fish, and more. The food in the Roux house was always good. We packed lunch for picnics in the summer: peanut butter and jelly sandwiches, Sprecher root beer, big bags of potato chips, cakes and pie. Some of my most cherished memories of Grandma and Grandpa and Dad on West Van Beck are the times we just laid out a blanket, opened folding chairs, and ate food in the park as we listened to a Milwaukee Brewers baseball game on the radio and threw a football around. There is nothing more powerful than a loving family.

I remember growing up on Van Beck across from Wilson Park. I remember the early '70s, we moved many miles east with Grandma and Grandpa to their new place on Carpenter Street. I changed schools again. And I ran into a whole new set of problems. On the good side, I remember the fishing and hunting trips with Dad, my brother, and my distant cousins. And I remember the ice skating and tobogganing all day on the coldest winter days of all and never being cold. I remember the smell of fires in fireplaces, burning leaves, the

Green Bay Packers at Lambeau Field, and when the
Milwaukee Braves changed their name to Milwaukee
Brewers.

Our childhood experiences shape us—the good ones and
the bad ones. If we take for granted the good and harp on the
bad, we can get lost because we are not dealing with truth.
Truth is reality. Nobody can survive in a fake world. One day
it crumbles and collapses, and you are left alone to pick up
all the pieces. Truth is the only way to have a chance at life. I
had good experiences and my share of lousy experiences
growing up. They shaped my interpretation of life. Not until I
lost my dad in 2005 did I realize how important he was to me.
When my biological mom dropped out of my life in 1966, I
was lost too. I needed a mom and a dad. Five years after the
divorce Neola wanted me to meet her new baby. That was the
first time she reached out that I knew about. Dad had
remarried. I knew God had answered my prayers. My new
mom seemed to love us right away. I loved her right away.
She helped fix me just by being there for me. And she always
told me the truth. I don't know who I would be without her
in my life.

6

"Home is the place where, when you have to go there, they have to take you in." —**Robert Frost**

Milwaukee, Wisconsin—1972 and onward

After we moved in with Grandma Kathleen in 1966, I did not see or talk again to my biological mother —Neola—until 1972, and that was the only time. She contacted Greg and me through my dad. Neola had remarried in 1971, and wanted us to meet her new baby, Sherry. I was ten. I remember feeling uncomfortable. I did not understand a lot of emotions, but I felt hurt because I thought my mother did not like me anymore. She had left and did not contact us for a long time. It was like she did not want to have anything to do with Greg and me.

Today, I still don't know how much of my memories of

33

emotions are real or have been made up over the years. Now that I have two children—Ryan and Kaitlyn—I cannot imagine walking out on them. Even after a divorce, I could never exit their lives. As an adult, I struggled to understand how Neola could. When you are a kid, you don't know the rules. Back then, I thought divorce meant someone leaves forever. I would find out more about that after Francine came into my life.

She was number fourteen out of seventeen kids. To add to the challenge, her father died in 1963 when she was only twelve. Francine grew up fast and lived in one of the poorest and roughest neighborhoods of Milwaukee during some of the most turbulent civil rights times in America. Francine was so poor she tied rags around her roller skates to keep them on. Every day she went to Goodwill to look for a better pair of skates for a dollar.

Growing up in the bad part of town was not easy, but she was a survivor. She was not afraid of work and had many hard, physical labor jobs. She made floor mats, worked in a lumber mill and made cabinet doors, and worked for the city school system. Francine was a liberated woman that did not need a movement. She always rolled up her sleeves and worked side-by-side with men, putting in long hours and long weeks.

She was an attractive lady and strong woman. Francine made it in life on her own. Even as a ten-year-old, I could see why Dad fell in love with her. My prayers had finally been answered. In September of 1972, Francine married Dad and I got a mom. I would not know until years later that she would be more than a stepmom. She was a best-friend mom.

In 1971, Dennis Roux met Francine Crisp between New Year's Eve parties. He was leaving one when they met. He offered her a ride to the next party. I guess something magical happened. Maybe it was love at first sight. They got married nine months later.

To add to the great news, Frannie had a son, Jeff. We became a blended family. Right after Dad and Francine got married, we moved out of my Grandma's house on Carpenter and into an apartment back on West Van Beck. Two years later, we moved to Greendale at Grange Road several miles south. Then, after a few more years, we moved back to the Carpenter Street neighborhood into a house across the street from Grandma Kathleen and Grandpa Larry.

Even though things were better—financially and family stability—there were some major emotional problems brewing inside of me. Five moves meant new schools (Greendale and Pulaski), and that meant conflict. I was stronger. I had a mom again. But being the new kid in school wore me down emotionally.

The kids and the cliques are not kind to new people. We are targets. To add to the difficulties of walking the halls between classes, and surviving lunch, new teachers, and courses were different. There were different rules, expectations, and grading standards. For me it was like starting all over again each time. It made school twice as hard for me. What once was passing in one school was failing in another school. And from my view the teachers did not care what I had to say about anything. I was just one more problem for them.

I got into a fight every day—I would not be bullied. Eventually, I gave up the relentless battle. I started to skip classes, and then I skipped school. To add to my hell, Dad was missing in action. And when he was around, he was asleep on the sofa. At the time, I had no idea what he was going through—I just felt he didn't care. Not until adulthood would I understand. But by then the damage was done. I dropped out of high school my senior year. I got my GED and joined the Army. A year later, I joined the Navy. Three years later, I followed a girl to California, got two jobs, and worked my way through college. I guess I was running away from high school all that time. Then something happened.

I stopped running.

The first reality check has to do with my biological mother, Neola. I thought she did not care about Greg and me. After the divorce in '66, I saw her once. She had a baby with another man and wanted Greg and me to meet baby Sherry. Because Neola was missing from my life for five years, I thought she did not care. It was not until I grew up that I learned the truth.

I am sure Grandma Kathleen had all the best intentions when she told Neola to leave the boys alone. Grandma said to Neola that, if she really cared about the boys, she would let them move on. Her presence would only confuse them. I think as an adult I realized Neola cared about all her children but that did not mean she could show it. I would not know everything for years.

page 36

Francine told me the truth after Grandma died, in 2012, at the age of ninety-six. I was in my late forties. Truth was that Neola cared so much that she did what Grandma told her to do. I know Grandma thought she was doing the right thing, but I have learned in life you never win when you manipulate truth. People get hurt every time. The love a mother and a father have for their children is powerful for a reason—the child needs it. Managing a divorce is no reason to manipulate truth. Guidance that kept Neola out of our life was wrong. Greg and I paid a price—a broken heart, anger, and insecurity for years. Our young hearts were damaged because someone stepped in and made things go the way they thought it should go. Once again, hiding truth is the wrong thing to do. Truth, even in the tough times, works. Truth is magic.

When I was a kid trying to figure out life, I wrongfully believed my mom did not love me anymore. I blamed myself. I felt I had done something wrong. Then came the next bomb. My father remarries and is gone from my life all the time. I am struggling in school and my dad is not there to help me. In my kid brain, I thought Dad did not care because my life was getting worse by the day, and he was nowhere to found.

Not until adulthood did I learn what my dad's life was all about. He did care. He cared so much that he worked sixty-hour weeks and twelve-hour days, ten days in a row to provide a home for us, in a chaotic world. The company he worked for in Milwaukee made automobile frames. Dad was a supervisor. I did not know his company was the world's first fully automated assembly plant capable of making one automobile frame every eight seconds—10,000 frames a day. Dad was in charge of a production line and a lot of people at a place the world recognized as a mechanical marvel! At age thirty-one, I went inside the place where my father worked.

Greg and I took the five-mile tour. In addition to managing a lot of workers on a production line, dad kept it running error-free and was the union steward representative —the precinct chairperson for thirty-five years! Dad was responsible for 3,500 workers and all of their problems. When he was not home after work, he was in arbitration for employees and the union.

When I struggled in school, my father struggled to keep a job. When I got into a fight, my father had to bring people together to solve problems. I was a confused kid only thinking of my problems and wondering where dad was. When he watched the news instead of throwing the football, I did not know he was learning about wage-and-price freezes and how it affected work. I did not know he was following the Arab oil embargo because it led to gasoline shortages and would hurt full-sized car sales and meant dad's work was going to make fewer car frames and dad would have to manage layoffs. He would have to handle union labor disputes and manage employee unrest. We had a ten-month strike I did not even know happened. When GM Motors promoted their new front-wheel drive cars on TV, I did not know it meant unitized bodies and dad's company would be making fewer car frames. While I was dealing with school, my dad was trying to change his production line to make truck frames to battle the foreign imports. I did not know every new car cost $30 million in retooling the assembly line. That meant people would lose jobs.

Later in life I learned all about the company and my dad's job responsibilities. When I did, I dumped a lot of childhood baggage. The truth set me free! Thinking for a moment that dad would rather work and watch TV than spend time with the family is absurd and false. Yet I manufactured that scenario and felt bad about it. If I had been thinking clearly, I could have dumped that miserable emotional load a long time ago. All the facts were there, but I missed them. Dad was busy trying to keep his job and help his workers and friends keep theirs.

Once again, truth made a huge difference in my life. Everything has meaning, but the truth is a required ingredient. Later in life, we figure out our teen years. Class reunions are eye opening. The high school football player and the most popular guys are not half as successful as the quiet guys who struggled with their identity. It is more proof that the teen years are full of untruths and incomplete perceptions. Some of us are good at fooling ourselves. Most of our crippling memories only exist in our heads.

The family can help if we listen. Our journey is not over when it starts. Our job is to be patient with a good heart and open mind so we can find our truths.

7

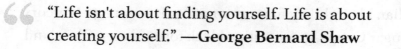

> "Life isn't about finding yourself. Life is about creating yourself." —George Bernard Shaw

1970s—Milwaukee, Wisconsin

I have come to think life is a combination of many separate journeys that seem disconnected but are not. During the next twenty years, I felt like I was wandering through a big maze. I was unsure of direction and purpose. I could be anywhere in this maze. I could be getting more lost. When I felt that way I stepped back and tried to take a broader look at my life. When I was in my teens, it did not help. In my twenties, it helped. I started to see there were separate beginnings, middles, and ends. When they started to connect, I saw I was blazing a trail... my trail.

Cudahy, Wisconsin is 4.4 miles from Wilson Park and

West Van Beck where I had spent many of my younger years with my grandparents and later with dad and Francine. Cudahy is a postage stamp size town. It is less than five square miles and has a population of maybe 20,000 people. It got its name from Patrick Cudahy. He moved to Buckhorn in the late 1800s and bought 700 acres and built a meatpacking plant. They named the town Cudahy. The meat packing plant still exists on One Sweet Applewood Lane. But that's not what brought me to Cudahy.

I got a job at a machine shop. I learned a lot and loved working with my hands, and I liked the people. I worked there from 1977 to 1980. Before the machine shop, I had a lot of different jobs. They were low paying, but I saved every dollar. I bought my first car for $800. It was a 1971 Mercury Cougar Coupe, green with a black top and a 351 Cleveland engine. It was my prized possession.

I loved working on my car and working at the machine shop making $5.25 an hour. I did not like going to high school. I always felt like an outsider. After moving to and from Van Beck twice, we moved again to Greendale and again to Carpenter Street. I went to Greendale High School 1976 and 1977, and Pulaski High School 1977 and 1980. Like elementary and middle school, I struggled with the changes. I had new teachers, a new grading system, changes in subject focus from one school to the other, new rules, new students (and cliques), and worst of all new expectations by teachers that did not know me. A passing grade in one school could be a failing grade in the other. I took courses over. They were completely new! Everything was different—

the people and the buildings and the hallways and the campuses.

I did not have many friends because I was the new guy, and my friends were scattered around in other parts of the city and other schools. The moves made it hard to try out for school sports. I did make the wrestling team but had to drop out when we moved again.

Soon, I started to skip classes, homework, and tests. I would skip early in the day and drive around and go to work. Then I started to miss classes on a regular basis—it went from days to weeks. I would rather be working at the machine shop in Cudahy or tinkering on my car. So, I dropped out. School was just not working for me.

I would get my GED—high school diploma—and join the Army, and Navy, and the day would come when I would go to college. My education path was atypical, but it fit me. I joined the Army in 1981. They sent me to Fort Benning for basic training where I decided I wanted to be in the Navy. I did everything they asked and climbed the ladder from Infantry to Navy Boatsman Mate, to Supplier, and finally to Radioman. I spent the rest of my four-year tour in the Pacific where I enjoyed and benefitted from the experience. I became a man. I learned a lot more about life and made lifelong friends. I accomplished the famous Shellback initiation—a recipient of a line-crossing ceremony. It is an honor bestowed upon the experienced sailors who cross the equator and return during their many sea journeys. It is a great honor.

When I got out of the Navy in '84, I followed a girl to San

Francisco and began a new journey. I drew upon my
maturing experiences in the military and realized it was time
for me to do something that would set a new course for a
better life. I wanted success.

I started to look for more than a job. I wanted a career.
Something challenging and respectable with a future.
Something that would allow me to eventually earn a good
income. I wanted to be a professional. I wanted to wear a coat
and tie and use my skills in a business atmosphere. All I
knew was blue-collar work. In the beginning, I worked for a
trucking dispatcher on the docks. It was a lot of heavy lifting
and sweat and aches. I worked my way up on the dock, but it
would not be enough for me long term. I also worked in sales
for an oak furniture store. This gave me an opportunity to
use my head and mouth more than my arms and back. I did
not see the job as long term either. I had started to look
around for something more.

There was a turning point in my life. I went on an
interview with US Steel in Berkley, California. It was and is a
strong company with a great reputation. I interviewed well. I
knew my interviewer liked me. We hit it off. At the end, he
told me to go get a college degree and come back—they
would hire me then. I said, "Give me ninety days and I will
outsell everyone." He said, "I think you probably could, but a
college degree is a basic requirement for a good job with US
Steel." That experience hit me hard. It resonated. It was
clearly the key to unlock the doors to the next level.

Soon after my US Steel interview, I was accepted at
Chabot College in Hayward, California. I started classes to

get my Marketing Degree. My military experience had a beginning, middle, and end. It was clear to me my Chabot College was the beginning of my next journey. I would do all I could to get my degree. I could not be swayed.

1987 was an important year for me in my process of evolving (growing up). I was in my junior year at Chabot College. Mentors are important in so many ways. A mentor is someone who had accomplished things in life that stops and reaches back to help others climb the ladder of success. Mentors sacrifice their time to make a difference for someone they believe is worthy and would benefit from their guidance.

In 1987, I met Don. He would be a mentor.

Don was one of my college instructors at Chabot College. One day in class, we talked about pros and cons, unions versus non-unions. I was independent. We debated. He asked me for my position and why—which one is best? My father was a member of the union all his life. He had been elected to a union leadership position—a Precinct Chairperson—by 3,500 union members, at the place where he worked most of his life. Still, I took the position independent is best. Don liked my arguments so much that he took an interest in me. He suggested I join DECA—the Distributive Education Clubs of America. I did.

In my junior year, I participated in the California DECA competition with fifty colleges. I won third place in state—the Public Relations category. The state DECA conference held in 1987 at the Berkley Convention Center was gratifying. As a state winner, I received a scholarship and later an all-expenses-paid trip to the National DECA Convention in New Orleans.

While holding down two jobs in the San Francisco area and taking classes at Chabot College, an ad in the newspaper caught my attention—the Conwood Company was hiring sales representatives. I don't know why this ad caught my attention, but it did. Conwood was a well- established, hallmark, national producer of fine chewing tobacco and snuff products sold everywhere. Their name brands were well known and well established: Kodiak Bear™, Levi Garrett™, and Grizzly™. Something told me to interview with this company even though I already had scheduled interviews with Hershey™ and Trident Gum™.

Something about Conwood drew me in. It was a feeling of completeness. It was like I had found the place that should be my home. I did not feel that way about Hershey™ or Trident Gum™, although I knew they were great companies as well. When I called Conwood to see about an interview, they were immediately interested in me. Conwood wanted to interview me right away. It just happened to work out that I would interview with Conwood before Hershey™ and Trident Gum™. It would not be until years later that I would find out the possible source of my special feelings for the Conwood Company.

I went on the interview. It went well. It felt like family. I was home. And the feeling was mutual. They wanted me right away. They hired me on the spot with one condition. I would agree to finish getting my degree. Wow! We were on the same page. I totally intended to get my college degree. It was good to know Conwood supported me. It became clear to me Conwood wanted me to be the best I could be. They knew it would be best for them, too. It meant a lot to me they believed in me enough to hire me while still pursuing my college degree. It meant a lot that Conwood would invest in me upfront. They showed me it was a two-way relationship. We both gave. They would take a chance on me. That was the type of organization I wanted to be a part of. Conwood would be my second home.

I know the combination of my personality, work ethic, military service, and unwavering pursuit of a college degree moved me to the front of the line with Conwood. But it would be several more years before I understood the less-than-obvious reason I found this company. They connected me even more to the bigger things that were coming my way. Going to work for a tobacco company took me to places I needed to be and opened doors I needed open to me. As I look back, it is clear to me I had a little help along the way.

8

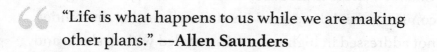

"Life is what happens to us while we are making other plans." —Allen Saunders

1987—Northern California

Life is full of surprises. I finally figured out you have to overcome the bad and you have to be ready to capitalize on the good at all times.

In 1987, at the age of twenty-six, I was responsible for 5,000 accounts in San Francisco, Oakland, and Sausalito. While I worked, I continued my studies for my college degree. I handled all sales and marketing responsibilities for the various product lines that flowed into retail outlets across one of the biggest markets in the country. To put my life-to-date into perspective, I had dropped out of high school nine years earlier!

Grizzly™ chewing tobacco was the Conwood flagship brand. Kodiak™ snuff was the most popular name brand in the premium snuff market. We also produced two more high quality brands of snuff—Hawken™ and Cougar™. Conwood was also known for its loose-leaf chewing tobacco. The most famous brand still today is Levi Garrett™. Later they added Taylor's Pride™, Morgan's™, and Peachey™. I remember going through orientation and training at Conwood to learn about these products and the marketplace.

My view of the classroom had changed since my high school days—I tossed the teenage problems into the Pacific Ocean while growing up in the military. Taking classes at Chabot College is probably when I found my learning comfort zone. I discovered I had some learning disabilities not addressed in high school. I struggled with dyslexia and more. Even in college it made learning more difficult for me. But I worked through it. I adopted the process of setting goals and working to them. I realized I did not have goals in high school, except to get out. Without goals, I had a lot of time to think about growing-up problems. And I had no help on my learning disabilities. I found the strength to overcome a lot on my own.

Orientation and training at work were another growth experience. I went into it with two goals. One, I would prove to the company that they made a good decision when they took a chance and hired me. Two, I would be one of their top sales representatives. Both goals were possible only by knowing the products and the markets and a lot of determination.

At the company's sales training class they began with their vision and values. I will never forget the powerful message. They talked about building a future of long-term growth success by focusing on the people responsible for developing, manufacturing, and marketing their products. I could not believe it. My world was evolving before my eyes. It was not that long ago when a lot of companies worked their people too long hours and too long days for profits.

Just like Don had a big impact on my growth and development at Chabot College, there were two mentors at work that helped me climb to success in business and as a person.

Don was an excellent regional manager and Hardy a great national sales manager. I remember Don taking time with me. He cared. He wanted me to be successful and did all he could to share the keys to sales success. I will never forget Don's three rules that guarantee success: (1) be patient, (2) listen to your customers, and (3) always follow up.

Hardy encouraged me to build high-profile relationships. I knew a lot of professional baseball players chew tobacco. If I could get close to some baseball stars, then our chewing tobacco products would get more attention by our retail outlets and distributors. I was smart enough to know I had to find a way into the baseball clubs that no one was using. I decided to focus on the equipment managers: I got to be close friends with some because I sampled chewing tobacco for their teams. As a perk, I got seats behind the dugouts and home-plate for customers at the San Francisco Giant games. I also got close to the Oakland Athletics

equipment manager. I was able to get baseballs signed by
stars.

Those were the days of Mark McGuire's rookie year, great
players like Jose Canseco, and Barry Bonds. I knew the
equipment manager with the Minnesota Twins, too. I think I
might have impressed my wife-to-be when I got some great
seats at the stadium. Hardy praised my work with the
professional athletes after he saw some baseball players
holding our tobacco in an issue of Sports Illustrated. That
was all my work! Over my career I worked with football
players too. I knew the equipment managers in the days of
the great players like Joe Montana and Jerry Rice, although
they were not tobacco users. Some liked the baseball caps we
gave out. Some even wore them on the sidelines at games.

Later in my career the government started to regulate the
tobacco industry. Unfortunately, sometimes good things
come to an end. My sample programs had to stop. I still had
great relationships, however. When I left the business, I was
always in the top 5 percent of the sales force and always
made bonus. I also had more than fifty baseballs signed by
the top professionals. I would give them to various charities
for fundraising events. I had a great career, lots of work and
lots of fun over the years. I believe, if you love your job, you
will never work a day in your life. I was lucky because I loved
working for that company.

In the early 1990s, I realized important things in life. I can
learn from every life experience as long as I am giving my
best and paying attention to details. My career was as
important to my development as my time at the machine

shop in Cudahy where I made $5.25 per hour. In Cudahy, I did not just avoid high school classes, I learned responsibility, trust, and reliability. I found I am capable of learning anything when I have a goal. I actually learned how to learn in that machine shop, and I would use it throughout my life.

My military experience taught me discipline and love of country. I learned how to build friendships based on common goals and trust. Nothing good comes without hard work. My father and Neola and Grandma Kathleen and Francine each invested in me their own ways. They shared wisdom and always meant well. My father taught me a successful life begins with God, family, and friends. Francine taught me to take responsibility. Grandma taught me to be sensitive and passionate and to find something bigger than me to believe in. And Neola introduced me to my Chippewa Indian roots. She said one day they would help me find my way. The Deer Stand Murders showed me life is unpredictable. It can be over in an instant through no fault of our own. That sad day, in November 2004, showed me there are heroes walking among us. It really opened my eyes.

While living in California, every summer, I returned to Wisconsin for a two-week break from work and quality time with family. In 1992, I would be surprised at how special the trip home would be. I would embark on a journey that would change the way I looked at the world and how I fit in it. Going into it, I would realize everything that came before— good and bad—had to happen exactly the way it did.

In '86, when my dad started to build a house on the Rice

Lake property he bought in '81, I did not think much about it. It was not that I did not care. It was that my life was on the West Coast. I had left the Navy and started college and had two jobs. I joined DECA (Distributive Education Clubs of America). It took my time, too. It would be another year before the Conwood Company would come into my life. Dad built a pier-and-beam ranch-style house with a cedar-wood exterior. The 2,000-square-foot house had a floorplan that handled family gatherings on the holidays. The house was on Minnow Lake. I remember the times we fished it over the years. Great memories.

I liked the place. I liked it so much I would buy it from Francine in 2006, just over a year after dad passed. It worked out best for everyone—Francine could use the money and we wanted to keep the place in the family. After I bought it, we updated and remodeled to suit our current needs. The three-bedroom-and-two-bath house with a nice basement and attic was just fine. We had a lot of good memories at the house on Rice Lake in Wisconsin. And we would build even more over the years.

In 1986, I did not know my life was about to go down a new path. It would start with an eagle encounter in 1992. I would return to my homeland and my roots and experience dreams, have visions, and learn more about the world around me.

9

> "There are two mistakes one can make along the road to truth; not going all the way, and not starting." —Buddha

1992—Milwaukee, Wisconsin

Sometimes the most unlikely events turn into some of the most important life moments. When I say I believe everything matters, I mean big and small. While living in California I would return to Wisconsin every year to visit family. Those ties were strong and very important to me. In the summer of '92, I went home as usual. I never felt bad about taking time off in the summer because my work closed the plant every year from the end of June through the 4th of July. It was the perfect time to visit. Before

55

this trip I got a letter from my biological mother—Neola. She wrote that the government owed my brother and me money.

An old treaty with the Mole Lake Ojibwe Tribe had been settled. There were checks waiting for us at the Mole Lake Reservation. Up until the letter, I had rarely thought about my American Indian roots. If the government wanted to give me some money, I would certainly be happy to take it.

Neola Roux (now Smith) gave birth to me on September 13, 1961, and my brother Greg on the exact same month and day two years later. She has always been a proud native American Indian. I did not know on the day of our births, Neola's father—a full-blood Chippewa Indian—enrolled Greg and me into the Mole Lake Ojibwe Tribe. We had our official birth records with the Chippewa Nation. They held our registered IDs, proof of our Ojibwe bloodline.

The first treaty with an American Indian tribe was ratified by the Continental Congress in 1778, during the Revolutionary War. The Continental Congress, composed of delegates from thirteen states, made a treaty with the Lenape (Delaware). This was the first treaty ever by the newly formed United States with an American Indian Tribe. Although it is not known for certain, most historians believe the United States entered into the treaty to either gain an alliance or commitment to neutrality with the Indians during the American Revolution. This treaty became the model for treaties with the Native American Indians.

It never dawned on me there could be an unsettled Indian treaty in 1992. Probably like most people I assumed treaties had been handled long ago. How could there be even one unresolved treaty in modern times? After a little personal research, I learned there were more than 370 treaties written and ratified between the Revolutionary War (1775-1783) and the Civil War (1861-1865). To my surprise, I also learned every single treaty had been broken, nullified, or changed, and it was not by the Indians.

The more I looked the angrier I got. Treaties were with individual tribes because they were viewed as independent nations with their own rights. The intent was to give value to the Indians for land as settlers moved westward. It was because of the large number of settlers and the relentless pace westward that the treaties could not adapt fast enough. They were ignored or unlawfully changed. These were dark days in our nation's history. But there were fair-minded people on both sides committed to fixing the problems.

President George Washington tried to improve relations with the Haudenosaunee Confederacy, an Indian nation composed of six tribes on the east coast: Mohawk, Cayuga, Onondaga, Oneida, Seneca, and Tuscarora. Washington returned more than a million acres of land wrongfully taken, and he committed the US government to make annual payments to tribes for the wrongs. The Ojibwe nation—of which I am connected by blood—is one of the tribes forced to leave their homelands. They were pushed westward. They resettled in north-central America and Canada. I have ties to the Mole Lake Ojibwe tribe in northern Wisconsin. The Treaty of Greenville (1795) provided the Ojibwe Nation with some resolutions but like other treaties it was broken. I never got all the answers. The

Mole Lake Ojibwe settlement was a long time coming. Financial remedies were a part.

I doubt many today fully grasp the extent of lawlessness and chaos during the formative years of our country in the 1700s and 1800s. Although it is shocking to learn there are unsettled Indian treaties today, a look at our history explains a lot. It has taken decades of legal actions to cut through government red tape. Settlements for generations of American Indians are happening. The Mole Lake Ojibwe treaty settlement included payouts to members of the tribe. Neola wrote that Greg's and my checks were waiting! Of course, it made perfect sense to visit the reservation during my family trip in the summer of '92.

On a sunny day, Neola and I drove from Milwaukee to Mole Lake, Wisconsin. The traffic thinned as we left the city and traveled into the wooded hills and valleys of rural Wisconsin. We got an early start. I wanted to get to the reservation early enough to take care of the paperwork, get our money and Ojibwe ID cards, and return to Milwaukee before dark. After hours of driving, we were on State Highway 55, the last stretch, Mole Lake Reservation was two miles away. We were alone, no cars and empty skies. Then we saw the eagle, in the distance.

In Wisconsin, seeing the occasional eagle overhead is not that unusual. This encounter began like all the others—a speck in the distant sky. Usually, a sighting is a fleeting brush with nature, like the occasional elk or bear and cubs on the edge of the woods. This time, when I saw the eagle, it changed course to me.

"This eagle has no interest in us," I thought. It was on its way to somewhere or something behind me. That's why it turned in the sky. What I thought would be another fleeting observation had changed. At that moment, I did not expect this eagle encounter to be much different. Maybe it would stay in view a little longer than usual. What happened next would be something I would think about often and not begin to grasp the significance for years. This eagle marked the beginning of another change in my life. What made this different was how this enormous bird abandoned a slow, meandering glide with a sharp and abrupt turn onto its new flight path, and I seemed to be the target. In a strange way, as I watched it approach, I felt like this eagle had been waiting for me. It saw me when I saw it. Then it adjusted its flight path onto a straight-line to me and never veered of it. As we moved down the highway at sixty mph, the eagle adjusted!

Maybe it locked onto something near to our car. Maybe it had food in its sights—a rabbit or a snake. Or maybe it found another eagle and moved into another wind current. I checked the mirrors and looked out all windows and saw nothing. We were very alone on an empty road and the eagle was very alone in an empty sky now descending on me at an increasing speed.

Then it leveled out just above the road. I've never seen an eagle fly this low right above the steaming tarmac. *What's with the laser-lock on my car? Has the color got your attention? Is it the sun reflection? Am I a shiny thing in the valley—a curiosity?* This encounter was crazy and awesome at the same time. Eagles do not get near cars, much less attack them. And eagles also do not fly low right above a roadway. We were going to collide!

It was only Neola and me and this enormous eagle. I stared in awe. It was the biggest one I had ever seen. The outstretched wings seemed to almost touch the edges of the road. It was like it could wrap its wings around the car. I watched as it effortlessly tilted left and right to hold its line while battling crosswinds. Without thinking, I let up on the gas pedal. We slowed. "Are you going to run me off the road," I wondered, half kidding and half not. "What are you doing?" I slowed more. It kept coming. One of us needed to do something. We were going to hit...

From the corner of my eye, I saw Neola's hand slide to the edge of the seat and squeeze. With her eyes locked on the majestic and daring bird, she stiffened. Her back pressed into the seat as if bracing for impact. I slowed more. The eagle held its course and speed. My thoughts screamed. *You're looking right at me. I see your eyes. You're locked on me. My God! What're you doing? What is this about? We're going to—*

I could not take it anymore. I pulled off the road and stopped and braced for a bloody impact. *You will destroy the windshield, kill yourself, and maybe kill me. There's no way you will survive this!* The giant bald eagle, with its powerful wings outstretched, hovered five feet above the tarmac. It adjusted course to my parked car. Neola froze. I gripped the steering wheel and pushed back in my seat. *It wants to die*, I thought. *But, why me?*

In a millisecond, the eagle tilted ever so slightly and zipped my side window, his white- feathered head cocked with his penetrating eyes on me. The huge shadow washed over the car. Neola and I turned in unison. We watched it make one more adjustment, and then shoot straight up. It had to be a thousand feet. In a chilling silence, we watched the tiny speck in the sky grow larger and larger as it shot back down and leveled at a hundred feet. From there it glided into the woodlands and disappeared. After a few long quiet minutes, and when the skies above the Mole Lake Indian Reservation were empty again, I crawled back onto the highway.

What just happened, I wondered as I rubbed the goosebumps off my arms? My mouth was dry. My heart beat in my throat. This was not just a big bird flying close to my car. I've seen some eagles in my life, but I have never seen anything like this. It was much more than just an encounter. It was a life-changing event! I felt it in my racing heart. But I would not understand anything about it for years. Neola, with her eyes straight ahead, said she knew exactly what happened. It was not her first. She smiled and turned to me, saying, "This is a good sign, Scotty. The great spirit welcomes you to my people."

I smiled with loving respect and silent skepticism. Throughout my life I heard about the Chippewa Indian traditions and spiritual beliefs. I knew they held a great respect for the eagle and Mother Earth. They believe the eagle is the greatest of all spirit animals. It is a powerful messenger from the creator to man. But, in the summer of '92, I was a successful businessman making a good living. My head was full of complex business knowledge of modern-day sales and marketing. I understood product life cycles and customer demand and market strategy. And I was a college graduate. I was a very busy man. I climbed out of the blue-collar world into the white-collar world. I thought I was so smart that no one could teach me anything. I had all the answers. An eagle is a bird. End of story.

When we drove onto the road and crawled the rest of the way to the reservation, I knew something important happened even though my head was not ready to process it. I was so into my business world that I could not begin to handle a foreign spiritual reality. I had room for my Catholic upbringing—that was it. I was nowhere near able to accept the unprovable spiritual explanations held by the Chippewa Indians. That day, I was only capable of feeling. Little did I know that powerful feeling would never go away. When I saw that majestic bird shooting toward me, I thought about my Indian blood. Maybe my ties were a bigger part of me than I had considered? Did the eagle come to me for a reason?

Today, I know that eagle came to me with two messages. I know that may sound like a stretch, ridiculous to some, because it did to me in the summer of '92. I did not understand because it was big, and I had no knowledge. All I could do was feel a door open. And I thank God I went in. I had to understand the new unknown. I wanted my eyes, heart, and mind open for truths. The eagle got my attention. I started educating myself. I studied the Chippewa ways. I set myself free from the limits of the modern, intellectual world where we think we know everything. In fact, I know we understand very little in this world. Only through spiritual eyes can we access the rest of it.

My day of understanding came many years later. I now know the eagle came to me with two messages—welcome and wake up. It did all it could to get my attention. And it would not be the last time. I would have countless meetings with the great thunderbird. In '92, I went to Mole Lake to get my money and I left with a key to my Ojibwe Indian legacy, a path to enlightenment. I would find the answers to my questions. And like most journeys in life, I traveled alone. Today, when I share my insights, I am often misunderstood or not believed. That is okay. In the summer of '92, I found my bigger-than-me thing.

10

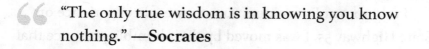

"The only true wisdom is in knowing you know nothing." —**Socrates**

1992—San Francisco, California

After my vacation in Wisconsin that summer of '92, I returned to California and my duties as a manufacturer's representative. I thought I would get back into my routine, but that did not happen. I was different. Something had happened that changed everything.

I still gave my 110% effort for the company, but I had something new rolling around in my head. As I worked to achieve my sales objectives and serve my customers, my thoughts returned to Neola and the Ojibwe reservation. Between sales calls, the same movie played over and over again. I really tried to think of other things, but I always drifted back. And the chills went down my spine—I could see the eagle gliding away. The very moment I found him with my eyes, he turned and came to me. In my dreams, I could see the eyes. I could feel the connection. Instead of the memory fading, it grew in intensity and I saw more.

I thought a lot about when Neola and I arrived on the reservation, how we went inside a building and met a lot of people. Neola's uncle greeted us. There were many others who knew Neola from childhood. I met members of the tribe and some of the most-respected Ojibwe elders. After the papers were processed, I picked up the government checks and Ojibwe ID.

I told some of the elders about my eagle experience on State Highway 55. I was moved by their humble presence that revealed a great wisdom. It drew me closer to them. I thought maybe these old Native American Indians that lived through a changing world had answers for me. These elders know of the great wrongs perpetrated upon their people over generations. I had to find out where they drew their strength. How do they cope with pain and disappointments, the endless struggles of their tribe? Maybe they could explain my experience. I felt it was more than an eagle sighting. Maybe the Ojibwe elders had some answers.

Each elder listened with eyes locked on mine. Each gave their undivided attention as if we were alone in the great room. When I spoke, I saw corners of mouths lift. Were they holding back because they thought me a fool, or did my words touch a memory? Either way, I knew they did not want to interrupt. I would learn the elders held back their smile like a father hides his smile as his son walks in snow for the first time. They saw I was suspended in between awesome and doubt. It was the place each visited and would not forget —the first spiritual connection. I would learn later they did not speak because my journey was to be a journey of one. Their smiles were meant to encourage. A gentle prod forward. Seek and you will find. At the end of that day, I had told my eagle story many times—one elder at a time. Each had the same words. Without pause and their eyes on mine, they said the thunderbird welcomes me into the Ojibwe tribe, and so do they.

For many weeks I pondered the words of the elders. I came at it many different ways and still reached the same place; either the eagle did exactly what the elders said, or everything they believed a lot of mumbo jumbo! But how could all the Native American Indians be wrong? For centuries they lived close to Mother Earth. Some say the population in Native American Indians exceeded twenty million. It is obvious to me they know what we do not know. I could not let go of my eagle. I had to find out what it all meant. My head was ready to explode, but my heart was calm for the first time in a long time. Then, I had an idea.

In 1987, when I entered a new business, knowing nothing, I did not know much about the company or their products. I did not know about their business plans, their markets, strategies, sales technique, or their customers. The San

Francisco territory was enormous. I did not know how to take an order, how to process an order, how to fix a distribution problem, a packaging problem, or a delivery problem. It started to all change after I began their intensive training program. Only after a lot of study and effort did I begin to amass the knowledge base from which to grow. It did not take long before I could locate and give correct information to my customers, provide reliable and high-quality services, promote my tobacco products, and begin to build my knowledge base to a level where I offered some value to my customers. Dedication to the education process opened my eyes. In the summer of 1992, I decided to do the same thing with my eagle encounter and my Chippewa Indian bloodline.

I started to read everything I could get my hands on about the Native American Indian, their history, beliefs, rituals, legends, mythologies, and lore. I studied the Ojibwe tribal history, their sacred beliefs, and their rituals. I wanted to know where it all came from and what it meant. Like my business experience, I knew I had to study to understand. I knew, in '92, I had to study the history and culture of the Chippewa Indian Nation, and specifically the Mole Lake Ojibwe tribe culture and spirituality. I have Chippewa Indian blood running through my veins. It mixed with my father's European ancestry. The more I researched my roots, the better I understood who I am. Only then could my questions be answered.

The Chippewa are one of the largest Indian nations living

on the North American continent. They have the fifth largest
population among all Native American tribes. In the United
States only the Navajo, Cherokee, Choctaw, and Sioux
surpass them in numbers. The Chippewa Nation is
composed of 150 bands. Most live in Minnesota, Michigan,
Wisconsin, and southern parts of Canada—primarily
Ontario, Saskatchewan, and Manitoba.

I found it interesting the Chippewa Ojibwe are known as
a sedentary tribe—meaning they do not move around. They
fish and hunt, and they grow and harvest corn, squash, and
wild rice, and they mine copper. The Chippewa lived in the
familiar wigwams often seen in westerns. Wigwams are made
of bark, strips of sod (grass), and willow saplings to provide a
skeletal structure. The Chippewa are also known for the
birch bark canoe and birch bark scrolls.

I discovered, historically, the Ojibwe were traditionally a
patrilineal system. That means the children were born into
the father's clan. Children born to an Ojibwe mother and
(let's say) a German or French father would be outside the
clan unless adopted by an Ojibwe male. Because Greg and I
are officially inside the Mole Lake Ojibwe tribe, the Mole
Lake tribe either does not practice patrimony, or we were
adopted. I was an adult when I learned from Neola that her
father handled Greg's and my paperwork with the Mole Lake
tribe at the time of our birth. I do not have the answer to the
question of practice of compliance or adoption that makes us
official members of the Ojibwe tribe.

Like other Native American Indian nations, the

Chippewa believe mysterious powers dwell inside all objects whether animate or inanimate. For example, they believe birds, rocks, rivers, mountains, fish, and trees have powers— and we are all connected in some way. They call this manitus. They believe manitus is alive in the summer and asleep in the winter.

The Chippewa also believe dreams are important. Dreams are conscious revelations with meanings. Dreams have messages for us. A manitus appearing in a dream can be a spiritual guardian revealing itself. This guardian watches over you. It helps you in your life.

After the summer of '92, the eagle started to appear in my dreams. Over time there were many different eagles in my dreams—bald, golden, normal sized, big, giant, and even baby eaglets. Once, I dreamed I had been carried by a giant eagle to its nest. I was dropped in with eaglets, then I awoke. When I learned about manitus and spiritual guardians, I started to wonder if the eagle could me mine. It seemed to have chosen me that day. Ever since that experience the eagle has appeared in my dreams regularly, and it has often visited me during my travels across the country. Prior to my amazing eagle experience, I rarely saw them. When I did, they were always far away.

In 2007, something would happen to me that would remove all doubts the eagle is in my life. On a cold winter day in Wisconsin, I met with an Ojibwa spiritual leader, Fred Ackley. It was the first time I had the honored experience. I had heard about this great man. Fred Ackley came from a very respected heritage; Fred is the nephew of a Sokaogon

Chief, Chief Willard Ackley, born in a wigwam on the shores of Bishop Lake on December 25, 1889. Fred Ackley knew about me. Later, I would learn he knew a lot more about me and my eagle experiences. This Ojibwa spiritual leader would be the one who gave me my Indian name.

After my first major eagle experience, I read everything I could find about eagles. I had never really thought about this bird before. Something inside drove me. I was interested in knowing more. I learned early that throughout the history of mankind the eagle has always represented great strength, leadership, and vision. I wondered, why this bird? Even in the Bible the eagle is often mentioned. Moses said to the Jews: "You have witnessed yourselves what happened to Egypt and how I used the eagle's wings to carry you." Moses described how the Israelites were protected by God who provided eagle wings to the people to gain strength and soar out of the reach of their enemies. The eagle has been used as the banner for many empires throughout history—Babylon, Egypt, Rome, Germany, and the US.

The eagle is important to the United States of America. For our nation, the eagle appears as a symbol of power and justice. It is our national emblem. It appears on government seals, our buildings, our currency, and coins, and more. This carnivorous bird, with a lifespan of fifteen to twenty years, a wingspan from six to eight feet, and a grip strength ten times more powerful than humans, is admired. The eagle's sense of hearing is as good as humans, but their distance vision is four-times better. Although this bird cannot smell, it has a perfect sense of taste. It will not eat anything that tastes spoiled, something that kills many wild animals every year.

US law protects the eagle from being hunted for its feathers. Only certain members of the Indian nations are authorized to kill eagles for ceremonial purposes. Eagle feathers are used in prayers and coveted gifts. The eagle is a spiritual animal to the Native American Indians who pass on their ideas and beliefs through signs and symbols with the eagle sitting on the very top of the totem pole.

The eagle, ruler of the sky, is believed to be the messenger connecting the highest spirit to man. It is said when one sees an eagle a prayer is answered, or message delivered. It may be an affirmation or spiritual guidance. And some believe an eagle encounter is a clear message to the one it visits—something is about to change and the time to be ready has come. It is the chief among the winged creatures, a sign of divinity.

The eagle reminds us, no bird flies forever, not even the greatest of birds. Each must descend to Mother Earth. Just as the eagle soars and reaches into the heavens, it too must descend to its home on the ground. Man can soar to great heights of accomplishment and understanding, but they too must be grounded, or they will die. When I connected with my first eagle on State Highway 55, I felt more than a big bird flying by. I felt a powerful connection. Only after I studied this spirit animal and its most honored position in Native American Indian rituals did I become ready for my journey —spiritual understanding.

One of the most powerful symbols I have found in

Chippewa Indian ritual are the eyes of the eagle. They speak of great vision—an eagle sees five colors, man sees three. An eagle can see a brown rabbit in a brown field a mile away. The symbolism has been passed down generations and is used to guide the thoughts and actions of millions. Like the eagle, we must see our objectives clearly from all sides and from far and near. When change is upon us, we have two choices. We can be like an eagle and adapt to change, or we can be like eagle's prey and be consumed.

I continued my study of the history and beliefs of the Chippewa Indian Nation, and I studied well beyond the eagle. The day would come, in 2007, when I would return to the Mole Lake Ojibwe Reservation—only 4,904 acres around Rice Lake, Bishop Lake, and Mole Lake, and today the home for only 500 tribal members. I would return to the place where my biological mother once lived and where the Ojibwe Indian still harvest wild rice and spear fish in the traditional ways. I would return to the place where the Indian lives in accordance with centuries of sacred trust in mother earth and spiritual grounding. I would return to the place where my Ojibwe Indian family exercises rights given them by the United States government through treaties. They adapt to change like the eagle.

I would return to the place where I would meet with Spiritual Leader Fred Ackley and receive a special blessing. I would take part in a sacred burial ceremony and be given my Ojibwe Indian name. I did not know in 1992, or the years that followed, how important my time with Fred Ackley would be. I would receive from this honorable man a key piece to my life puzzle. I would receive powerful confirmation that I was on the right track with my journey. In 2007, I would learn the giant eagle had chosen me on that summer day in 1992. In the ceremony, Fred Ackley would reveal to me the eagle is my manitus.

11

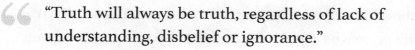

> "Truth will always be truth, regardless of lack of understanding, disbelief or ignorance."
> —W. Clement Stone

Summer of 1992—Milwaukee, Wisconsin

1992 was a pivotal year and a long way from the Deer Stand Murders in 2004, the death of my father in 2005, and my jaw-dropping meeting with Fred Ackley in 2007. The 1992 eagle encounter on State Highway 55 set the stage for the next two-decades of my journey. There were many other events along the way that aided in my growth. The eagle encounters kept moving me forward in search for answers. Some encounters seemed normal and others bizarre. In time, I would see they all were part of an unexplainable force pulling me into a new awareness.

During those two weeks back home, I did more than visit the Ojibwe Reservation to pick up my government check. My father arranged a tour for me and my brother at his old company. At the age of thirty-one, and an experienced businessman, I would now get to see the place where my father spent most of his life while I was growing up.

I heard the name of the company around the house as a kid. I would hear my dad say it when he was talking to Grandpa Larry and Grandma Kathleen. Back then I had no concept of work. It was the place my dad and Grandpa Larry went during the day and a lot of weekends. It was the place they came from when they were late for dinner. It was the place where dad was when I had a problem I wanted to talk about, and when I just wanted to throw the baseball. Work is the place where you have a boss that you complain about. Sometimes you're so mad at the boss you want to quit the job. Work is the place where you really do not want to be but must be. They make you do things you otherwise would never do. But work pays money to do things. Now, when I think about it, it is ridiculous how a kid thinks. I don't remember anything before age five. My memories start around age six. I remember thinking work is that thing I will have to do one day. It is like school. I will have to put up with bosses like teachers.

I did not start really putting things together until age twelve. It was not that I did not get the concept of work. It was that I never thought that much about it. When the word work came up, someone in the family would be talking about Grandpa Larry or dad. It always sounded like there were problems they needed to fix, and about something stupid the boss made them do. And I remember they never got paid what they thought they should be paid. I assumed work was a dark, unfair place you were forced to be at.

Work meant money. I always did things for money, things I would do on my own like mow my neighbors' lawns, deliver newspapers, rake neighbors' leaves, shovel neighbors' snow. I really got a grip on the concept when I got a job in the machine shop at Cudahy. Instead of the job being something I did not like, and something anyone could do, I realized work can be fun. You can bring (and develop) skills and do things not all people can do. I realized the more I worked on my skills at the machine shop, the more I was appreciated and paid.

When I made good money and enjoyed my job at the machine shop, I realized it was very possible to get another job I liked in the future. A job that would pay me a lot of money. I realized I could grow with my job. I realized if I stuck with something I could get really good and be in demand for some special skill. As a teenager the benefits of work started to get real and motivating. I purchased my first car. I impressed the girls. I had money to take girls on dates and to buy things I wanted. I did not have to ask my parents for money or permission. Looking back, I am sure my teenage view of work led me to where I am now.

Unlike the kid on Van Beck and Carpenter, things were very different for me in 1992. I was thirty-one, a Navy veteran that had sailed halfway around the world, a college graduate, and a successful manufacturer representative with a big job on the West Coast. I had gone through several training programs. I had mentors and friends and business associates. I had customers that were happy with me and customers that wouldn't give me the time of day, but I had to find a way to make them like me so I could sell them my products. That was my job—sell chewing tobacco and snuff products in the city of San Francisco and surrounding areas. Sell products one way or another, or I could get fired. The company had objectives. They were paying me to help achieve those objectives.

When I came home in 1992, I was a grown man. I understood work very well. I came home knowing dad worked all his life. Dad was a responsible and reliable man. He worked long days and long weeks doing back-breaking work in a modern manufacturing plant with thousands of employees and hundreds of deadlines. I came home knowing, like me, my dad had good days and bad days, and, like me, he had to perform, or he would get fired. Money would stop. Life would change. I also understood my dad had two jobs. He was also a member of a labor union and served as an officer on the Grievance Committee, Local 19806.

Dad worked at one company from the late 1960s to his retirement in 2000. When I went on the two-hour tour, I could appreciate some of the workings of the manufacturing facility because of my business experiences, but I was not prepared for what happened at my father's workplace. Like the eagle on State Highway 55, this experience with Greg and dad at the big manufacturing facility in Milwaukee blew me away. I was not only in awe of the size and complexity of the car-frame manufacturing plant, but I was also moved by all the employees I saw on the tour and the overflowing respect they showed for my father. I think almost every one of the 3,500 employees at that plant knew and thought good things about my dad, Dennis Roux.

I mentioned earlier that the plant in Milwaukee was the most modern manufacturing facility for automobile frames in the world from the 1960s into the 1990s. This assembly operation, from start to finish, was three miles long. Every ten seconds a new car frame rolled off the line. Although I could see it with my own eyes, I could not rationalize how many things had to happen perfect to make a car frame every ten seconds. I had a tobacco production background. I understood harvesting a crop, cleaning and cutting tobacco leaves, packaging, and labeling. There was simply no comparison to the complexity of this operation.

I was told it was a mechanized process with more than five hundred separate operations feeding the main production line. To produce 10,000 car frames a day everything had to happen on a split-second timeline. One error could stop the whole operation. Talk about pressure. Pieces of the car frame moved from many different inventory locations onto a side bar press line or a similar conveyor longer than a football field. Many of the different pieces were manufactured at the plant. The assembled frame passed through washing machines and painting machines, and then hung on a chain where the frame was lacquered, baked, and cooled. Each car frame was made with more than 125 parts assembled in forty minutes.

We got to walk through the plant and see the different stages of the car-frame production. Then it happened, I learned more about dad. The things kids never realize because they are too busy thinking about their problems or baseball or girls. Everywhere we went people yelled out to my dad. They said, "Hey, Gomer... Hey, Roux-man... You are the man, Roux." There were posters all over the plant with my dad's face and the words—ROUX IS FOR YOU! Dad was the union precinct representative. He was chairman of the Grievance Committee for many years.

At times, I felt like I was in a Rocky movie. The constant calls to my dad were unbelievable—as if he were a movie star. I think just about every worker waved, or smiled, or yelled out to him. Most yelled out: "Vote for Roux, the man! He's the best!" Dad ran every year for the committee position. Union members vote. He won every year but two.

It was obvious to Greg and me that our dad had come a long way from his starting position as a common laborer. It was not easy to be a chairman of the union's Grievance Committee. He had to deliver. During times of great civil unrest across the country, and strikes, and layoffs, my father must have done a lot of things right for a lot of people. Eighty percent of the workforce were minorities—African American —and they chose my dad. They respected him because he respected all people regardless of race or status in life. Dennis Roux would be the union's precinct representative and a committee officer up until his retirement in 2000.

The tour of my dad's workplace, in 1992, was important to me for many reasons. Like the eagle encounter, I became aware of things I had never thought about while growing up. We all get so busy with our lives that we forget to open our eyes to see what is really going on around us with the people that raise us. We carry a lot of half-truths around. If we don't open our eyes, we can wake up one day and realize we missed everything important. After spending time with my dad on a tour of his workplace, I got a closer look at the man who raised me.

How can Dennis Roux be seen by 3,500 employees as a fair man, who cares about their problems, yet I have memories of him as a kid as being someone too busy to care about helping me with my problems? Well, of course, my childhood point of view is wrong. It is not reality. The score is 3,500 to 1/2. Dad cared about my problems. I am his own flesh and blood. As an adult in '92, I had neatly tucked away in my head a flawed view of my father. Although it was not something I consciously held against him, it was something I carried around that affected how I thought and acted. Unconsciously, it affected all my judgments. The tour opened my eyes to my flawed view of my dad. I realized my father lived a life dedicated to caring for other people. When I thought about that reality, I thought about all the times we talked. Dad did try to help me grow up. I just didn't listen—a typical kid.

The tour experience was another positive catalyst in my life. I got to see my dad through the eyes of others—the people who spent a lot of hours, days, and years with him.

The people who depended on him and voted for him because he was good. They saw what I had missed as a kid. They saw what I had yet to reexamine as an adult, but then my eyes were opened.

Personal growth is about opening your eyes to get things right. Each step forward matters, and a lot of steps turn into miles. It determines if we are to be complete or incomplete people—happy or sad, empty or full. My eagle encounter on Highway 55 and my tour, put me squarely on the path I would travel. I would learn not to fear truth, even when I do not yet understand. I would learn to eliminate lies and errors in interpretation. Often it is easier to hold onto them because they are familiar. But they serve no purpose. They hold you back. I realized truth is the only way to the answers I seek.

12

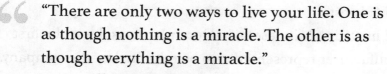

"There are only two ways to live your life. One is as though nothing is a miracle. The other is as though everything is a miracle."
—Albert Einstein

1994—Bloomington, Minnesota

I had to return to my roots in 1994. The spirits pulled me back to my homeland.

Almost two years had passed since my amazing connection with the eagle. After that eye-opening visit back home, I began my research of the Chippewa Nation and my Mole Lake Ojibwe roots. The more I learned the more it spoke to me. I would think about it day and night. It was in my dreams. My head seemed to align with my heart for the first time. Although business was doing well, I felt unsettled and out of place. Something tugged at me. At the time I did not understand much. There was one thing I did know. I was not supposed to be on the West Coast anymore.

I was supposed to be in the Midwest.

I had to go back to the Wisconsin and Minnesota part of the country. While in San Francisco, the more I learned about my Native American Indian roots the more I was pulled. In the winter of 1993, I decided to go back home. I wanted to spend quality time with my dad, and I thought about starting my own business. My work surprised me when they gave me a call to offer me a transfer anywhere in the Midwest.

I moved to Minnesota, in December 1993. I was the first manufacturer representative to be relocated by the company. The company paid for my move back home and carved out a new territory for me. When I look back, I should not have been too surprised. I left the San Francisco territory I had built from nothing, and it took eight new part-time sales representatives to fill my shoes. I left a good thing but deep down something told me the move back home was right.

Looking back, I got ten more years with my dad!

They were great years, too. We hunted and fished together, went to baseball and football games together, went to church together, and talked about everything a father and son could talk about. Those ten years were my most important. Dad and I were not only close as father and son, but we also became close friends.

My work did all they could to keep me with them after the move. I had developed a number of successful sales techniques. One brought the company valuable exposure in professional sports. I knew some baseball players chew tobacco. So, I got to know the equipment managers for the professional baseball teams in my territory. I free sampled them some products. After a while, they treated me like a part of the family.

After I relocated to Minnesota, I connected with the equipment managers with the Milwaukee Brewers. My sample program was appreciated by a lot of the baseball players, team managers, and even owners. Our chewing tobacco got some great exposure. On occasion some teams would give me complimentary seats right behind the dugout! I would take other customers to games and sit near the pros! On occasion, an athlete would sign baseballs and give them to my guests and me. My professional sports sales strategy worked well for everyone. My sports success really came from my personality and selling skills. The company did not want to lose me.

My Native Indian blood coupled with my '92 eagle encounter led to a lot of new things in my life that are connected. For example, my research of the other American Indian Nations was eye-opening. I discovered most, if not all, Native American Indian rituals and sacred beliefs are shared by most tribes. There are a lot of unique rituals and special treatments of course, but the basic ceremonies are very close.

All Indians communicate with Mother Earth and the great spirits.

While still in California, I was surprised to find eight tribes in the northwest part of the state. Although most are a fraction of the population they once were, they had survived massive change over the centuries. Today, they remain true to their ways. They celebrate life through their sacred rituals. For example, the world-renewal ceremonies practiced today have changed very little. They still are intended to prevent natural catastrophes—floods, fires, earthquakes, and crop failures. They have ceremonies to protect health, their food supply, and homes. The rituals have not changed over hundreds of years. I thought it was funny how I sold tobacco products that the Native Indians love so much and use at rituals and ceremonies.

In northwest California, there are many tribes (Tolowa, Karok, Whilikut, Chimariko, and Wiyot). When I could, I traveled to Indian reservations as a representative of the tobacco company. I knew from experiences in Minnesota that many Indians enjoy tobacco. I was always welcomed and I always made friends. After all, I sampled chewing tobacco. This was a great opportunity to better my sales goals, as well as learn more about Native American Indians.

Something new happened when I started to visit Indian reservations. It got to be routine. Every time I went to or returned from a reservation, an eagle visited me. That held true in California, the Dakotas—when I visited the Sioux reservations—and later when I relocated to the Midwest and visited the Arapaho, Cheyenne, and Crew reservations. After

'92, I knew we (me and the eagles) were building a relationship. One that I may never fully understand or be able to explain. But it was something real.

My Native American Indian visits to give free samples chewing tobacco were different after my 1992 eagle encounter. Prior to that experience I did not see many eagles. After the encounter, I was visited all the time, but they aren't exactly like the '92 experience. Each time the eagle made its presence known and then left. Sometimes, I noticed one flying nearby and I was thinking about something else. In those cases, the eagle would pass over a second time but closer. It would look at me in my car. It was like it needed me to acknowledge its presence. After I did, it would fly away.

In the past, I saw an occasional eagle. After '92, I started to look for them. If I did not see one, I would get a little worried—did something change? Then one would fly into view. I got to where I expected it. I started to believe the eagles were watching over me. But still, my first eagle encounter was different. The first one was not watching over me. It was delivering two messages. One I was sure about. Welcome to the Mole Lake Ojibwe Tribe. Not until 2006 did I know the second message it delivered that day.

After I relocated back to the Midwest, I felt I was where I needed to be. I was comfortable with my territory south of one of the largest Midwest dual-city complexes, Minneapolis-St. Paul. I went to work right away; I wanted my company to know they made the right decision supporting my move. I wanted to show them I would work hard to exceed my sales objectives with existing accounts and new accounts. Two things I learned from my father were to: be productive and always put in an honest day's work. I saw myself as a member of the team, with common goals.

That year the dreams started. I could recall every detail. I dreamed about eagles flying into the sun and returning to earth. I watched them land on fat branches at the top of tall trees and the edges of cliffs. And I saw them look off into the horizon as if they could see everything. As if they watched over much more than I would ever know. In my dreams, they always turned their heads to me. I always saw their penetrating eyes and their noble stance. I felt if they could smile, they would.

I was a single man all my life. Although I dated many incredible ladies, I did not meet the one I saw as the mother of my children. In 1995, I was still a bachelor. I think Dennis and Franny worried about me not getting married but said little about it. Marriage was okay, but I needed to find the right person. A traveling salesman is not the easiest job to marry into. I was traveling and living out of a suitcase 70 percent of the time. When I was at home, I was exhausted. One night after a long day I fell asleep early and slept like a rock. That was the night I did not dream about eagles or my Indian heritage. That night I visited a church in my dreams.

I had no idea why I would dream about a church, but I did in 1995. I was a good Catholic boy, so I assumed I dreamed about a Catholic Church. The one in my dream was new to me. I had never seen it before. I was driving in the middle of nowhere, a vast treeless prairie. I don't even remember seeing crops—typical corn or wheat or sorghum. I just saw miles of empty land covered in short grass like a tundra. All of a sudden in my dream I came upon a church. It popped up out of nowhere in the vast, empty land. It was early morning, the end of winter or beginning of fall. The sun was blinding but not hot. No clouds in the sky. The only trees were around this church. I saw beautiful ice crystals on the trees and the manicured lawn.

I was amazed at the detail of my first church dream. When I awoke, I could remember the details as if it happened. I even remember seeing the steam coming up from the grounds as the sun poured over the frozen setting (from the night before). In my dream, the church was a combination of brown brick and rock and splashes of cement near its base. The roof was steep and there was a steeple at one end. I could see the teal aging on the copper steeple. Beneath the steeple was a square brick structure sitting on top of the church. I could only see one side. There were two shuttered windows. They were long and narrow and rounded at the top like some of the other windows on the main part of the church beneath the steeple. This church was very distinctive. It was long and narrow and a relatively small church, and it was nestled in the only trees I could see in the middle of an otherwise treeless landscape.

For the longest time I could not fathom why I would dream about a church I had never seen before. Then, almost one year later, I met the girl I dreamed about in 1995. I had never seen the girl before and I had never seen angels in my dreams. But this was the girl I would marry.

I met my wife-to-be in the spring of 1996, in Maple Grove,

a small town in Hennepin County, Minnesota. Yes, I met the girl in my dream. And yes, I was shocked and confused. Did I foresee this? Did I have some ability I had not yet recognized? Is this something coming out of my Native American Indian research and blood? At the time, I did not want to tell her about my dream. After all, it sounded a little creepy. I didn't want to chase her off before I got to know her. Then, a year later, 1996, I drove to Benson, Minnesota, to meet her parents. Our relationship was getting serious. We had fallen in love and marriage was in the cards.

On my trip to Benson, I experienced another significant eagle event. Although I had seen eagles on the road to and from reservations, this one was very different. It was a lot like my 1992 experience.

I was traveling down Highway 12, about thirty minutes outside Benson, Minnesota, when

I saw an eagle soaring on the horizon. It was far away. Like my '92 experience the very moment I found the eagle it turned sharp and came straight to me. But this time, instead of passing by the car a few feet off the ground, this eagle got a few car lengths away from me and shot straight up and away. It must have stayed out of my line-of-view on purpose because, after it shot up, I never saw it again, and there was not a cloud in the sky. It was almost as if the eagle did not want me to see him (or her) leave. Was it sitting on my car roof? Somehow it managed to avoid me as I looked out each window and all my mirrors. The other thing it did, like the one in '92, was fly close enough for eye contact. This eagle looked into my eyes. And then it was gone.

I kept driving. The rest of the way I was a little unsettled. Then I remembered all my eagle encounters have been good signs for me. This time I was on the way to meet my future bride's parents. Maybe this eagle's message was confirmation good was coming my way?

I would marry on October 11, 1997, at a nearby Catholic church selected by her family. When I went to see the church in Danvers, Minnesota, west of Benson, the hair on my neck started to stand on end. I drove the familiar road although I had never been on it before. The surroundings were in my dream two years earlier, a tundra-like setting.

There was not a cloud in the sky that sunny morning in March 1997. Then, there it was! I tried not to react visibly. I did not want to startle anyone. The church in my dream popped up out of nowhere. The 200 block of Washington Avenue. It was built with brown-brick and stone. It had the steeple in my dream, the windows and teal-green stained copper spire. The church was long, narrow, and small. There were ice-crystals on the trees and the manicured lawns. The steam was coming up as the morning sun turned the night frost into water. I saw the Church of Visitation for the second time in my life.

As I approached the property, I swallowed hard. Although I was trying to hide my shock, I was also curious. How could I possibly know the church one year before I had even met my bride-to-be and two years before I would be married in it. How did I dream about a church in such detail, one I had never seen before?

This private experience is something I will never forget.

As I learn more about my Ojibwe roots, I can see there are far more things in the world that we do not understand. I told very few people about this dream because it was hard enough for me to rationalize. The day I traveled to Benson and met my wife's parents I was unsure of where everything was going because I had never been married before. Her parents were very polite, very religious, and very good people. They lived on a farm where they grew beans and corn. They loved their farm life. I remember at the time I felt this was where I needed to be. I felt lucky to be with so many wonderful people.

We were married eight months later, October 1997, in the church I had visited in my dreams. Three short years later Ryan Christopher was born on Valentine's Day, February 14, 2000, and Kaitlyn Marie blessed us with her arrival on February 5, 2002. Before my beautiful daughter arrived, I dreamed she was a girl born on the same day as Ryan. Because we wanted them to have their own birthdays, we induced labor early. Although our marriage did not last forever, it did last a very long time and during some of the most important years of my life.

13

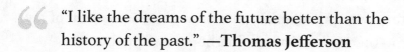

"I like the dreams of the future better than the history of the past." —**Thomas Jefferson**

"Live as if you were to die tomorrow. Learn as if you were to live forever." —**Mahatma Gandhi**

2000—Rice Lake, Wisconsin

My father retired in 2000. He sold the house in Milwaukee and moved into the house he had built in Rice Lake in 1986. By the year 2000, my life had settled down. I had survived the transition from California to Minnesota. I had safely returned to my homeland and got married. On February 14, 2000, our son Ryan was born. The next month, we moved into our new house in Minnetrista, east of Minneapolis-St. Paul.

Everything was perfect. Even my job was going well. I had built sales in my new territory, reaching or exceeding my company goals. They were pleased with my performance and their decision. Just as they had supported me in the beginning—hiring me before completing my college work—they supported me on relocation. They took another chance on me by financing my move from California and carving out a new territory.

I will never forget the year 2000. Many good things happened to my new family and me. I was especially happy with my job. They treated me well throughout my career. I am sure they knew I could never let them down. The only negative was my travel. Unlike San Francisco, my new territory was spread out. I spent more than 60 percent of my time on the road and a lot of nights away from home. Overnight travel was not bad when I was single. Married with a kid is different.

I did not like packing my bag Sunday nights and putting my head on a different hotel pillow every night the following week. Although I missed my family, I had to accept travel as part of my job. After all, I was making good money and my eagle encounters were happening on a regular basis.

I was visited by so many eagles that it was almost predictable. As soon as I started to take it for granted, the skies over Minnesota and the Dakotas were empty. I would make my sales calls and begin to worry—where are the eagles? Was I imagining everything—I thought the eagles were watching over me? Then it would happen; another one would pass over me that day.

I can't prove it, but the timing was always perfect. It would happen when I got humble and felt insecure. It was almost as if they were teaching me to never take them for granted. I know that sounds crazy to some people reading my story, but there are a lot of days I experienced eagle visits right after I ate some humble pie and apologized to an empty sky.

In most Native American Indian cultures, the eagle is a medicine bird with magical powers. They have healing powers and are the most widespread clan animal used by Native American Indians. Why do so many in touch with the spirituality of Mother Earth believe? They say everything is connected and they place the eagle on a pedestal. This bird has touched the heart and soul of several hundred million Indians like no other animal on earth. They can't all be wrong. There must be something to it.

The American Indians believe one reason an eagle appears is to put someone on notice. The eagle instructs strength and courage at times of danger or confusion. Another reason an eagle appears is because it is watching over a person. If an eagle scares or attacks someone, it is said the eagle is telling them they have self-imposed limitations they need to get through—they cannot put it off any longer. Who am I to say an eagle passing over means absolutely nothing?

Who am I to deny the wisdom and experience of millions of American Indians who once governed this entire continent for thousands of years, longer than us? We must learn to accept things we do not understand. The longer I

live the more I know how little we know. The arrogance of
man throughout history has always been a weakness. When
will we learn we are a part of something much bigger than
we can possibly imagine?

The power and spirituality of the Native American
Indians is hard to explain to people when they have no
knowledge and even less interest. We get set in our ways. It is
unfortunate so many will miss out on an enormous piece to
the puzzle of life. There is a whole world outside of the
iPhone, mainstream media, and the political world we live in.
Too many today treat science and technology as a god. They
get all their trusted information from untrustworthy sources
and wonder why they do not receive confirmation or
satisfaction. I have found most of what happens in our world
is unexplainable. It just is. If you have any hesitation, I
recommend you read about and listen to some of the greatest
minds in history. Hear what the people with the highest IQs
have to say. Read about Albert Einstein, Nikola Tesla, Isaac
Newton, Leonardo DaVinci, Galileo, Stephen Hawking,
Charles Darwin, Benjamin Franklin, Aristotle, Thomas
Edison, and Socrates. They know more than anyone alive
and yet they admit to knowing very little. They say the
arrogance of civilized man has done humanity a disservice. It
keeps us from knowing all that we could know in this
amazing world.

I started to grasp the importance of the eagle when I
invested a lot of personal time to learn as much as I could
about the Native American Indian, their life and culture.
These are the people most in touch with the world we live in.

They have a reason to love, respect, and praise the land, the wind, the water, and everything alive and everything not alive. What is it they know? They believe the Creator has a reason for everything and everything has meaning. The Creator even placed secrets in the rocks for a reason we must try to understand. The Native American Indians believe everything in the world is connected and dependent upon all other parts. When one part is affected, another part is affected. When I see the enormous respect they have for the eagle—in their rituals, prayers, ceremonies, totems, paintings, headdresses, and jewelry—it is only natural to conclude the Native American Indian knows more about the eagle and how it fits in this world than anyone else.

I have Ojibwe blood and am a member of the Mole Lake Ojibwe Tribe. The Ojibwe are an Algonkian-speaking tribe and the largest single Indian group north of Mexico. They call themselves Anishinaabeg which means the true (or original) people. It was the Europeans and other Indians that called them Ojibwe or Chippewa. These terms mean puckered up. It comes from the moccasins they wore. The Ojibwe first connected with European explorers in the early 1600s. As the settling process began, they were pushed westward. Along with other tribes they went to war against the Iroquois who wanted to control the fur trade. The Ojibwe managed to win in their area around Lake Superior and the mouth of the Mississippi River, primarily Wisconsin, Minnesota, and Central Canada. The Ojibwe eventually allied with the French militarily and economically up into the 1660s. Indian wars lasted into the 1800s. The Ojibwe settled in Wisconsin in a place named Lac du Flambeau. The name means, "Lake of flames." The Ojibwe speared fish at night using torches attached to their birchbark canoes.

In the 1840s, the United States government decided to remove all Ojibwe Indian tribes from northern Wisconsin! The aggressive action ignored all existing treaties and all prior concessions of the Ojibwe Indian Nation that allowed them to remain in their homes in Northern Wisconsin. Several Ojibwe Chiefs went to Washington, DC, to beg President Zachary Taylor to let them stay in their homes. Taylor refused to even sit down with the Ojibwe chiefs! However, after Taylor's death in 1850, new President Millard Fillmore met with the Ojibwe chiefs and agreed to a treaty (1854). The Ojibwe chiefs agreed to give up the last of their lands in Minnesota, and President Fillmore agreed to four Ojibwe reservations in northern Wisconsin: the Bad River, Red Cliff, Lac du Flambeau, and the Lac Courte Oreilles.

After the Treaty of 1854, the Ojibwe did not have enough land to survive the old ways—fishing and hunting. They were forced to meld into the new ways. Their treaties gave them the right to fish and hunt on all ceded lands. But conflict arose. They were harassed and boats burned. They went to the courts where they were offered millions of dollars to stop fishing and hunting on ceded lands. They rejected the offers and faced constant harassment. Today they stock the lakes with more walleyes than they take out by spear fishing. The number of fish the Ojibwe take out of the lakes is small compared to the numbers taken out by sport fishermen.

When I learned this about the Ojibwe Indians, I was both saddened and frustrated. I love my country but am not happy with some of the things we have done historically. My purpose for sharing this information is not to demonize America, it is to educate more people on the less-represented portion of our society today. The Native American Indian has moved over and given up a lot. They lived on this land for thousands of years, and a lot has changed over the last three centuries. Since the Native American Indian has lost, we, too, have lost. They have much to bring to our nation including their rich traditions and sacred beliefs. I can promise special things to all who visit the hidden world these fascinating people cherish in all they do.

14

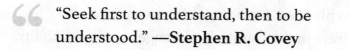

"Seek first to understand, then to be understood." —**Stephen R. Covey**

2003—Rice Lake, Wisconsin

I t was one year before six hunters would be murdered in the woods at Rice Lake in 2004.

November 22, 2003, the opening day of deer season a year before, I attended my first deer drive. By then, my eagle visits were frequent and often predictable before a special or potentially dangerous occasion. I did not share my beliefs with anyone.

On a cold November morning in 2003, no one saw the eagle but me, and I did not point it out. I watched it glide just feet above the treetops a hundred yards out. It landed on the tallest tree on the edge of the woods. This time the message would come sometime later.

Six hunters had arrived for the 2003 morning deer drive. I knew most. Some would be shot November 21, 2004. Some would live and some would die.

Some of the hunters were busy getting their hunting gear and guns ready. Others were drinking coffee and telling tales. I think it is the biggest part of the tradition, the comradery and the hunting tales before and after the drives.

I was nearby listening and watching the skies. I was looking for an eagle. Based on my experiences, I wanted to know how the day was going to go. Deer drives are potentially dangerous. Someone can get hurt if things don't go the way as planned. I was expecting to see an eagle because we were in the country and danger was a possibility. I started to worry. If I did not see an eagle, that would be a bad omen.

Now, looking back at the 2004 Deer Stand Murders, I wonder if I had gone and had not seen an eagle, would I have said anything? Would I have warned the hunters of an impending danger? Would I have trusted my unprovable feelings enough to speak up? I guess I will never know. And maybe it is a crazy thought anyway.

If I had said anything, I doubt anyone would have listened to me. Native Indian rituals and beliefs, and my very private eagle experiences and beliefs would not be enough to overcome opening-day traditions. I would have probably been laughed at— what kind of nut believes an eagle can foretell the future?

People have been hunting deer for centuries. Wisconsin deer hunting has been regulated since 1851. It evolved from the unlawful massacre of deer to the thoughtful management of a large and growing deer population. Over the years there have been changes in laws regulating the sport. Today, there are almost a million licensed deer hunters in the state. But like everything else in life, there are people for and people against. Finding common ground would take decades of discussions and experiences.

The first Chief Game Warden was appointed in 1890. Five years later, Sheboygan was the first county to close deer hunting. Many counties followed suit. In 1900, twelve hunters were killed by firearms. In 1914, twenty-four hunters were killed and twenty-six injured. More hunting guidelines and gun-safety regulations followed. In 1925, the Wisconsin legislature passed a law closing deer season on alternate years. Then there was a push for no deer season. Because deer have few predators (the timber wolf for example), the rapidly growing deer population had to be managed—they were destroying crops. Hunting was the only viable way. Soon, the closed counties opened (Walworth, Waukesha, and Jefferson) for deer hunting. By 1970, there were 500,000+ licenses sold, and 72,000+ deer killed with no deer-hunting fatalities. By the year 2000, the deer harvest climbed to 528,494 with 694,712 licensed gun hunters.

2003 was like every other opening day in Wisconsin. The 2003 deer drive went forward without incident, but I talked to friends and hunters who would die the next year! I wish there had been a way to avoid the tragedy of 2004.

In 2003, my distant cousins had invited me to join them
for the deer drive at Rice Lake. Although I had hunted
before, I had never participated in a deer drive. I thought I
knew enough about it, but after I saw how much of a big
production it was, I was really surprised. A deer drive is a
hunting strategy: it's like a team hunt, an alternative to sitting
alone in a deer stand or walking alone in the woods tracking
a deer. A deer drive involves more than one hunter, and it can
be effective in moving deer out of hiding. It can also be
dangerous because there are a lot of people walking around
with guns. There are chances of crossfire. If a hunter on a
drive does not do what they are supposed to do someone can
easily get shot.

A deer drive can be composed of a lot or a few drivers
moving deer to posters. Usually, deer drives are limited to six
or eight hunters at the most. The drivers encourage deer to
move from cover into an area where posters (the shooters)
wait. It may sound like a simple process, but if one person
does not follow instructions, deer can run wild or shooters
could get excited and shoot into unsafe directions.

The drivers spread out but stay within sight of each other,
typically twenty to thirty yards apart. They move the line
slowly toward the posters on the edges of the zone (fields and
woods). Everyone is positioned, coordinated, and should be
doing what all agreed to do. The posters wait for the deer to
be flushed out of the cover. Posters are not supposed to shoot
in the direction of a driver. Everyone wears fluorescent-
orange hunting coats to help reduce the chance of error.

In 2002, in the State of Wisconsin, there were 317,888 deer killed by 618,945 licensed gun hunters. There was another 54,133 deer killed by 227,124 licensed bow hunters. That means one in seven people in the state of Wisconsin is a deer hunter and less than half of the hunters bag a deer. The big numbers confirm a lot of people in the state love the great outdoors and the hunt whether they shoot a deer or not. Each year the numbers grow. Deer hunting traditions are cherished by 15 percent of the population, including my family. Although I did not hunt much, I enjoyed the traditions when I did. It was a great opportunity to be with friends and family in the beautiful woodlands of Wisconsin.

When I arrived in 2003, I joined my cousins. My brother would not be able to make it. He had a great excuse. His wife was delivering a baby that day. Believe it or not Pat, a distant cousin, showed up to the deer drive after the baby was born. The weather was perfect—not too cold, no rain or snow, and sunny without a cloud in the sky. Everyone was getting ready for the deer drive. Instructions were given, and then there was a lot of banter and friends poking fun at each other as they sipped hot coffee from their giant thermoses. I realized a lot of money and effort is invested by a lot of people to be properly equipped and skilled for nine hunting days a year.

I lost count of my eagle encounters after 1992. Before that year I could count them on one hand. Something happened on the road to Mole Lake that changed everything. By 2003, I was not only expecting an eagle to come to me. I had learned how to interpret their messages.

According to Indian lore, when one sees an eagle and the eagle sees them the message is the first clear thought. Sometimes it is hard to capture the complete thought before it is lost. A partial message, or unclear message, is no message. The head must be clear. That day, in 2003, I watched my eagle on the top of the tree a hundred yards away. I could see it had its back to me. No message could be sent until it found me. Maybe there would be no message that day.

Then the eagle's head pivoted to me. It was too far away to see its eyes, but his head now faced me for almost thirty seconds. The message I received—it will be a good day. Then it jumped off the limb. Its wings unfolded and flapped several times as it lifted up and disappeared into the woods. I said a prayer. In November 2003, the deer drive went forward without incident.

I cannot prove the eagle I saw foretold the future. I can say it landed and turned to me and my feeling was good— safe. And I can say there have been other times I've seen an eagle and my feelings were different: sometimes empowering, sometimes cautionary, and sometimes peaceful. I will always wonder if I had gone to the 2004 deer drive would I have seen an eagle. Would it tell me there would be danger? Would it protect me? Well, I may not have been at the 2004 deer drive, but my father was there and so was David. I learned these two men did see an eagle that day! It was not until 2007 when I met Fred Ackley that I would learn the eagle in 2004 was only seen by two men. Fred Ackley said the eagle protected my father and David, on that horrific day. Those two men drove into danger when the shooting began. They brought out the injured and dying. My father helped the wounded as he sat in the open bed of a pickup truck. Bullets flew but none found my father or David in 2004.

15

"Death ends a life, not a relationship."
—**Mitch Albom**

2004—Mole Lake Chippewa Indian Reservation

Totem Poles are Native American Indian monumental carvings we all know about. There is a reason why the Great Eagle sits on top of many. Totems symbolize cultural beliefs and commemorate ancestors. Totem is Algonquian (Chippewa) for kinship group. All totems tell a story. They recount legends and reveal clan lineage. They can welcome visitors and/or be mortuary vessels with remains of ancestors inside. Because of the symbolism and Native American Indian meanings, observers' knowledge is vital. If we take the time to study the eagle, we can understand our encounters. Why have the

Native American Indians glorified this bird? Without their knowledge the message from the eagle can be missed. I believe if we study the science and spirituality of the eagle, we have a good chance to connect with them when they are in the area. I truly wonder if they know who takes an interest in them.

Before I could even begin to appreciate the spirituality of the eagle, I had to understand the bird as a creature on earth. I wanted to know how the eagle is built. How can it fly so high, reach speeds up to 200 mph, and physically do such demanding tasks like catching prey and flying away with all the added weight. To do that the eagle's body must be strong as well as lightweight. The wings are the most important part of their body. They allow them to speed down on prey, take off with a heavy load, and land safely. The eagle is such an efficient and effective hunter, unlike other animals it spends little time hunting.

Their bones are hollow and very strong—mostly filled with air. There are braces inside the bones and on parts of the skeleton to add strength. Although eagles look big, their entire skeleton can weigh less than a few pounds, a small percentage of its total weight.

The wings are incredible by design. They are big, strong, and lightweight. The average eagle's wingspan is eight feet and only weighs two or three pounds. They have 7,000 feathers. The overlapping of the feathers leaves a lot of room for air to help with lift. In direct comparison to an airplane (designed by man), an eagle wing (designed by God) is much stronger. The eagle's wings allow them to stay high for hours at low speeds. The wing design also allows them to achieve great speeds as they descend on prey, and then slow for a safe landing. The total weight of an eagle can vary between four and fourteen pounds based on age.

The wing-flapping muscles are different. The muscles that push down are the biggest and strongest. They provide lift and determine flying power. These muscles can count for up to half the eagle's total weight. The muscles that pull the wings back up after the downward thrust are much smaller. But they are very important, too. They allow for safe landings. Eagles tend to choose dangerous places like narrow cliff ledges, tops of trees, and a jutting rock above the water surface. The upward wing-lift muscles allow for hovering, slowdown, and final touchdown on a targeted spot. If they could not consistently land safely, they would crash and perish.

Often, when you see an eagle or big bird moving in circles, they are doing one of two things. They are circling prey, or they are looking for a thermal. Thermals are pockets of warmer air. They exist over areas like dirt fields, parking lots, buildings, and roadways. Because warm air rises, eagles (and other birds) find them to help fly with less effort. The warm air gives them lift. The eagle uses thermals to ride up to great heights like airplanes. Thermals can also make for a bumpy ride when the flight path cuts through them in a straight line. That fact it is why I pay special attention to an eagle that turns and comes to me on a straight line. It is not a natural path. It is a choice. The eagle could be hunting, mating, or en route to a very specific location. Or the path taken could be a spiritual mission, one by this recognized spirit animal.

Knowing the basic anatomy and natural behavior of eagles (and basic rules of flight) can be helpful in determining when an eagle is on a mission. Like most birds of prey, eagles fly solo. They hunt and survive, on their own. They are the complete predator. There is no logical reason for several eagles to fly in formation a few feet above an empty road. They do not hunt in packs. Remember, they fly for very few reasons—to get somewhere, to mate, and to hunt. The day before we buried my father, Francine and I watched four eagles fly in formation a few feet above the road to our house, in Rice Lake. Why? I believe they honored my father.

Eagle encounters around my father's death were many. It became routine. We were all moved by so much activity. It reminded me of my Highway 55 experience. The eagle did not just casually appear. It went to great lengths to be seen. I will never be able to prove it, but in my heart, I knew that eagle's mission was to wake me up—and it did.

Two weeks after we buried my father, in March of 2005, I returned to my home in Minnetrista, Minnesota. My brother Greg stayed with Francine at the Rice Lake house for two more weeks. We did not want Francine to be alone right after burying her husband. One morning, two weeks after my father's funeral services, an unfamiliar noise outside got their attention. The noise came from the side of the house. Franny and Greg looked out the window and saw a swarm of bald eagles! There were more than they could count. They were stunned by the sight. Franny had never seen anything like it over her nineteen years at the Rice Lake house.

We know eagles are solitary birds with large hunting territories they aggressively defend against other eagles. Therefore, is it possible these eagles gathered for one of the very few known reasons? Did they gather because there was an abundant food supply—like a salmon run? I doubt it. Minnow Lake next to our house is not known for salmon. As a matter of fact, there is not enough fish in the small, thirty-five-acre lake to feed even a couple of eagles for long.

I do not think the old saying—birds of a feather flock together—applies to eagles. However, it was the end of winter—late March 2005—when they gathered on the grounds next to our Rice Lake house. And it is a fact some eagles fly south for the winter and return in the late winter and early spring. It is possible these eagles were returning to their habitats in the northern Wisconsin and central Canada area. It is possible they took a different return route. And yes, it is possible they stopped in Rice Lake for a short rest before completing their journey.

The gathering could have been related to migration. The only problem I see with that theory is eagles have never stopped at Minnow Lake. Based on what I have read, migration routes and animal (bird) habits are consistent and predictable. It takes something big to alter it like the weather. However, the weather in the Midwest in 2005 was typical. There were no big storms or temperature swings. Therefore, I do not believe weather altered these eagles' migration route. There are only a few other possibilities. One—they gathered in Rice Lake for no particular reason. Or two—they gathered in Rice Lake to honor my father. I believe it was number two.

I think I could have answered the question for certain if I had been there that day. I would have had access to the eagles and the message sent. Although I cannot prove it, and I could be wrong, I believe they gathered on a spiritual mission. Too many of nature's rules were broken that day. Lone predators—raptors—do not gather in residential areas. The danger is too great, and the behavior is too odd. They were not there because food was plentiful. And it could not have been some casual change in an established migration path. Never before have eagles filled the side yard. I believe in the unknown. We cannot explain everything in life. There are times you go with what your heart and your head tell you. This is one.

16

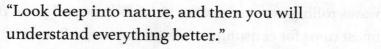

> "Look deep into nature, and then you will understand everything better."
> —Albert Einstein

March 2005—Jamaica & Rice Lake

We had to get life back to normal. The days and weeks after the tragedy in the Blue Hills at Rice Lake would never be the same for a lot of people, especially my father. He lived through the most horrific experience of his life. Dad rode into hell to rescue the wounded and dying. Bullets flew as they tried to get them out of harm's way. He said prayers over them as they rushed for emergency medical care.

After months had passed, we knew my father had changed. He did not want to go outside anymore. And he did not want to be left alone. That was not my father. Frannie said Dad asked her to take medical leave so she could stay home with him. At the time, we still did not realize how bad it was for my dad. We did not see the extent of his invisible wounds; not until it was too late, my father died three months after the Deer Stand Murders.

The March 2005 trip to Jamaica was planned before the Deer Stand Murders. I saw vacation promotional pieces at the Rice Lake house. I know they talked about going to a lot of different places for a 2005 vacation. They settled on Jamaica probably because the promotional pieces were so effective. Jamacia, the most precious jewel of the Caribbean with its glorious sunrises, sugar-white sandy beaches, gentle waves rolling over teal waters, rich food and song, and the finest rums for consumption as the sun is swallowed by the ocean. After the shootings I think they both saw the vacation as a chance to escape the ongoing nightmare for my dad.

My father wanted to go to Jamacia, but maybe not for the right reasons. Maybe he was running away instead of running to. I thought he was getting better. We all hoped he would adjust to the tragedy at some point. We hoped his desire to go to Jamaica was a sign he was getting better, getting back to his old self, enjoying his retirement.

I did not know his health had declined. Frannie told me Dad was not going to his doctor like he should, and he was not taking his meds as he should. Dad had heart problems, but they were manageable. He needed to eat right, exercise, and take his meds. I think Frannie thought the Jamaican vacation was what he needed. She saw how the shootings hurt him—the anxiety, the depression, and the paranoia. He really worried the shooters were coming for him next.

It did not help that the trial would not take place for another two years. No one got closure. There were no clear explanations or a resolution. The line between reality and wild imaginations blurred as the days turned into months of no clear answers about the shooter and the reasons. The newspapers covered the shootings, but their articles got into too much theory, speculation, and sensationalism. As the legitimate news reports waned, the uncorroborated stories grew. The coverage of the shootings remained incomplete and misleading. The truth and the facts were often lost in the mainstream media's sensationalized story lines.

The news seemed to frustrate and aggravate those who were there that terrible day. I think the circus around the shootings fueled the paranoia and fears. Like war stories, the incident in the woods was carried around by the eyewitnesses. They had to live with the terror and pain. And they did not want to talk about it with anyone. They suffered alone. I believe they did not get professional help because not enough people understood what they were going through. I believe my dad suffered with PTSD.

Dad died in Jamaica on March 7, 2005. The cause of death on the death certificate was cardiac arrest—heart attack. It took a week to get him home. They respectfully transported his remains with prayer and crosses. The funeral was held in Dobie, Wisconsin, on Monday, March 14, at the Lady of Lourdes Church. At Sunday Mass the day before the burial, they honored Dennis Roux—a good family man, a Carnegie

Hero, a man who now walks with God. I will never forget the gathering of people that came to honor my father and give their respects.

I will never forget the eagles. They came, too. Eagles were with us throughout our sad occasion. They came before, during, and after Dad's burial. I already mentioned the day before the funeral when Francine and I watched eagles fly in formation to the house. I will never forget those four eagles. It was so far beyond natural behavior. And I will not forget the road to the cemetery the day of the burial—I counted six eagles in a tree by the cemetery and five eagles on the side of the road; they made their presence known. I felt the eagles were honoring my father. Did the six eagles coincide with the six deer hunters murdered? I believe they did, but I will never be able to prove it. The message delivered to me was the great Creator was taking care of my dad. Still, as his son, I would think about him.

The Ojibwe Indians see the eagle as the king of the sky. It creates a path between our physical world and our God. The Ojibwe have believed this for hundreds of years—the eagle delivers messages from our creator. I have spoken a lot about the messages received. I have not shared that an eagle encounter can be something else—it can be an affirmation. For example, I say a prayer—God watch over my family— moments later I see an eagle. It appears to me out of nowhere. I believe that is an affirmation. I believe that eagle confirmed to me that my prayer has been heard. I have also asked for guidance and have been visited immediately. I believe the Ojibwe Indian Nation knows the true power of the eagle.

Ever since 1992, I have known eagles are special. At my dad's funeral thirteen years later, I knew it even more. I had studied the Native American Indians and the eagle. I wish I had been with my father on November 21, 2004. Because I was not, I will never know if I could have helped. I do believe I would have had a much better understanding of my father's condition three months later. I believe Dad died early because of PTSD. Most people only think of PTSD as a military condition. We must wake up the world. PTSD is a condition faced by millions of people every year as they struggle to live through personal, local, regional, or national disasters that hurt them—invisible wounds.

17

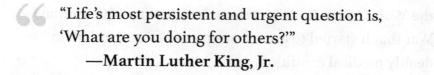

> "Life's most persistent and urgent question is, 'What are you doing for others?'"
> —**Martin Luther King, Jr.**

The three words—scared to death—are very real. Mass shootings are defined as three or more victims of firearm-related violence in a public place. It excludes gang killings, domestic violence, and terrorist acts. The Washington Post reported 163 mass shootings in the United States between 1967 and 2019. But the FBI reported mass shootings account for only 0.2 percent of all homicides each year. That low number does not include the true impact. What about the related PTSD deaths across the country?

In 2004, there were three mass shootings: the March 12 Fresno-Wesson shootings, the November 21 Deer Stand

Murders, and the December 12 Columbus nightclub shootings. In 2019, fifteen years later, there were nineteen mass shootings. This form of violence has increased, but there is something worse going on. The total victim count is more than those found dead at the crime scene. People related and unrelated to the victims, near and far from the crime scene, are victims too. We now know hundreds, if not thousands, of people suffer from related PTSD.

Post-traumatic stress disorder (PTSD) is partially understood today. We are familiar with the condition as it affects our military men and women, victims who suffer from a traumatic experience on the battlefield. Although PTSD has always existed, it was not understood during the times of the World Wars. It was not until decades after the Vietnam War that it started to get attention as a serious and often deadly medical condition.

The general public learned most about PTSD as a mental condition some soldiers suffered with upon returning from conflicts in the Middle East—Afghanistan, Pakistan, and Iraq. We became aware this mental condition was about the recurring and intrusive thoughts from the battlefield. Stricken soldiers suffered with terrible nightmares and daily flashbacks. They had anxiety, delusions, depression, and paranoia. The military victims of PTSD had little or no control over their nightmares or flashbacks. Some committed suicide. Some committed homicides as they relived their delusional moments. PTSD can lead to mass shootings.

For too long we only saw PTSD as a condition affecting military people. Today, we know this debilitating disorder can affect people in the private sector. The human emotions of fear, depression, anxiety, and paranoia are conditions that can arise from any and all traumatic experience—an automobile accident, house fire, loss of a family member, and much more. People still do not realize PTSD can exist in their community and even their family. Our human mechanism for coping with tragedy can be strong, fragile, or broken. A victim of PTSD left unattended can spiral out of control and put at risk their life and the lives of those around them. For example, the Galveston Hurricane, in 1900, killed 12,000 people. This was not an act of war. It was a tragic event that also hurt untouched families and the public across the whole country. Many suffered from PTSD. They were left untreated. Their premature death could have been prevented. We saw an increase in suicides and homicides from these terrible natural tragedies.

The North American drought in 1989-90 hit half the country and killed more than 17,000 people. There were terrible heat waves, dust storms, and wildfires. Many believe the unmeasured death count due to untreated PTSD was in the thousands. The trauma the survivors went through, the loss of loved ones, property damage, loss of crops and livestock, took a major toll. Many more thousands died from PTSD months later due to untreated depression and anxiety.

The same could be said about the 1906 San Francisco Earthquake. More than 3,000 people died, but the recorded numbers do not include the thousands of survivors that lived through the aftermath—fires and devastation. Almost 80 percent of a city was destroyed in one day. Ruptured gas mains lit up buildings across the city. There was widespread looting and riots. Thousands of people in that city were injured—physical and mental. We know many thousands of people suffered from PTSD. They had the invisible injuries that left untreated do not heal. In 1906 we did not know about post-traumatic stress disorder.

Anyone alive today knows the date September 11, 2001. Over 3,000 people died that day, in New York City, as the Trade Towers fell. And more died when heroes forced a highjacked plane to crash in a field in Pennsylvania. And some died when another plane hit the Pentagon. Not only did these tragic events kill many on that terrible day, but it launched decades of war in the Middle East and started hate crimes against Muslim people. Many lived in constant fear from that day forward. Everyone was touched by 9/11. The tragedy created a new population of PTSD victims—people afraid of Muslims, war, and terrorism. We all had to cope with something we did not fully understand. Many could not handle it. They lived injured. Some committed suicide. Most struggled to manage their hidden pain, fears, anger, distrust, paranoia, depression, and constant stress. Many just gave up on life. PTSD is real and dangerous to our society. It is a medical condition we understand but still do not look for. It is time to open our eyes.

Hurricane Katrina, the Oklahoma truck bombing, the assassination of JFK, the Challenger space shuttle explosion, and serial killers are examples of recent tragedies. The United States and the world have disasters all the time. People that die at the scene are reported in the death tolls.

We now know that number is an incomplete statistic. There are always far more deaths connected to all tragedies. Those who die later. They do not appear in the death toll. They are lost and we have an incomplete picture. We learn nothing. And to make it even worse, many of these people could have been saved. They are the people without physical injuries. And they don't talk about it.

We can see a physical injury. Even when emergency medical care is not readily available, we can help the victim stay alive until help arrives. It should be the same for a victim of PTSD. We each should know enough to recognize the disorder and help until medical treatment comes. Today, too often the victim of PTSD and those around them do not see the injury. They can't help. The victim suffers and often dies. I know this firsthand.

The 2004 Rice Lake mass-shooting tragedy touched me —my father was there. I knew most of the hunters shot. Back then I had heard about PTSD, but like most I associated it to the military. That day, and for many months after, our attentions were on the physically wounded and the dead. It did not dawn on anyone there were people with PTSD. I knew my father was shaken up, but I did not think about it as a medical condition needing treatment. I did not connect the dots—deer-stand shooting equals battlefield trauma. Today, it looks like an easy connection to make. But it is not.

My father, although undiagnosed, exhibited many of the symptoms of PTSD. He had nightmares and flashbacks. For months after the shootings, he avoided people and places. He wanted to stay in the house. He had trouble sleeping. Dad would sit by the window and watch. He was paranoid. It was just not him.

I think Dad may have felt guilty because he did not die that day. Because he survived, he somehow blamed himself for not doing enough. Although he and my cousin drove into the woods under fire to save people, my father grieved over what went on in his head. He was scared. In his head, he hesitated. In his head, he probably wanted to run away—*if I go in the woods I will die*. But in reality, Dad did not hesitate. He pushed back his fear. He jumped into the back of the truck and rode into hell. He risked his life. To this day, I do not know what he did in the woods—he never talked about it. I only know Dad returned with the wounded and the dying. I know PTSD has nothing to do with what happened. It is the aftermath—fear driven.

Now I know he relived it every day. That was not good for his heart. The paranoia grew. Dad had never been paranoid about anything, not until the 2004 mass shootings. Frannie told me he said he was afraid they were coming for him next. She never got an answer from him on who they were or why. The thought is irrational. Still, my father believed it.

After PTSD is diagnosed by a medical professional, the treatment plan has been shown to be successful in a lot of cases. The first thing the patient needs is help in changing their thought process. In my dad's case, he would have benefited from the guidance of a professional to help him through his nightmares. Help him see what really happened and what he really did. Someone could have helped him understand the reality of the moment and could have showed his positive role in a bad situation that scared everyone, not just him. It is called exposure therapy. It is the treatment process managed by a doctor that helps the patient relive the traumatic incident in a controlled and accurate way. Exposure therapy helps the patient understand and leave behind the false memories. It shows the patient that they are a victim, too. They have serious injuries. Like setting a broken leg, the development of coping skills to handle a tragic event is vital. The PTSD patient needs to see their injury as real and coping skills like a cast for a broken leg.

I know Dad would have benefited from the diagnosis and treatment for PTSD. Therapy alone may not have been enough. Sometimes medication is also required to manage depression, anxiety, and paranoia. The fact my father was not taking his cardiac meds is another indicator of PTSD. The lack of self-care is a form of self-punishment. Subliminal message: I don't deserve to live! After the 2004 shootings, my father did not take his heart medications consistently, and he did not go to the doctor as he should. This is another signal. I wish we had recognized it.

As I tell my story, I think about my decision to leave California and move back home in 1994. My father died three months after the 2004 Deer Stand Murders. What if I had not been here? Because I believe everything happens for a reason, I go back to my 1992 eagle experience on Highway 55. That life event did exactly what it was meant to do; I returned to my homeland and got ten more years with my father. We had some of my most cherished moments. Those years were important to my growth and development as a spiritual man. I cannot imagine what my life would be like if I had not spent those ten quality years close to my father.

I lost my dad on March 7, 2005. I learned about PTSD too late. I know my father suffered from this terrible disorder, although it was not diagnosed. Although I cannot help him now, I can help others by telling his story. I can raise awareness. If we know what to look for, we can get people medical attention and, when appropriate, treatment. Not only can lives be saved, but the quality of life can also be saved by shining a light on these invisible wounds known as PTSD.

18

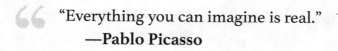

> "Everything you can imagine is real."
> —**Pablo Picasso**

April 2005—Minnetrista, Minnesota

We buried Dennis Roux on March 14, 2005. I returned home to Minnetrista, Minnesota. The orb visited me in early April of the year. It had a message. It was from my father.

I had heard about orbs but never thought much about them. I know the Ojibwe Indians believe spirits move in orbs for different reasons, some good and some bad. I had never seen an orb in my life, not until April 2005. It came into my bedroom through the closed window. It moved around the room, and then came to me.

People believe different things about orbs. Most agree

they are energy. They have been called ghost orbs, spirit orbs, and paranormal orbs. Although there are a lot of theories about this energy form, those who have seen them say they sparkle like a foggy, fizzling star inside a transparent ball. Orbs come in all sizes and colors. Some are captured in a photograph and others are experienced. They dart around and can pass through walls, trees, and people.

The skeptics say orbs are explainable. They say they are dust on a camera lens or gas or a reflection. This may be one way to explain away a given orb on a given photograph, but it does not explain away orbs that visit people with no camera lens to confuse things. Firsthand experiences are not easily explained. Not when a fizzling orb zips into your life, darts about, hangs there a while, and zips out of your life.

Scientists who think they have debunked orbs on photographs are unable to come up with viable explanations for most actual experiences. And they cannot explain the various behaviors of orbs or the wide array of colors: white, red, pink, orange, yellow, gold, green, blue, purple, brown, and even black. The Indians and paranormal experts have explained it. Orbs are not new to the Native American Indians who unlike others are well connected to the spiritual world. They do not rely on science for all their answers. I, too, do not minimize or ignore science. But I know science is not a perfect process like others may think. Skeptics rarely embrace new things in life, much less anything spiritual in nature, because they cannot prove it. Some things cannot be proven, especially spiritual things. The simple fact is there are far more unexplainable things and events in our world than the explainable.

I saw one orb one time. There are numerous cases where people see several at one time. They see orbs of all sizes moving in different directions at different speeds, coming and going. Seems to me that would be a hard thing for dust or gas to do. Multiple-orb experiences occur most often in secluded wooded areas, churches, graveyards, haunted locations (houses), and places where clairvoyance is practiced—like séances and Ouija boards and paranormal tours. Orbs also appear where death has occurred. One of the most well-known places for multiple-orb sightings is the battlefield in Gettysburg, Pennsylvania.

Orbs have been described as halos, ghosts, and angels of the dead. Many believe orbs represent energy patterns of these entities. An orb can contain the energy from one or more entities. Most believe orbs are spirits of deceased loved ones and angels. When an orb is spotted in a family photo, some believe it is a family member visitation from a different plane.

When my family returned home to Minnetrista, Minnesota, after my father's funeral, we sank into an expected depression. Dad was only sixty-three. We lost him too soon. I thought a lot about the Jamaican vacation, the place where Dad died. I remember at the time I thought the trip was a good idea; he really wanted to go. I thought that was a good thing. Three months after the terrible shootings in Rice Lake, maybe the trip would help him get back to normal.

I watched him change after the shootings. He got quiet, did not want to go out or do much of anything. When he showed interest in the Jamaican trip, we all thought it was a step forward; he was on his way back. After he died, I reevaluated. I had a lot of windshield time driving back home. The trip home is when it clicked. I think PTSD killed him! But then it was too late. We couldn't do anything about it. Then I started to think about Dad's afterlife. What else did I not know before it was too late, I thought? What if Dad needed something from me, now? I missed PTSD. I cannot miss anything else.

I wondered, "Where are you now, Dad? Are you in purgatory being cleansed of your sins? Do you need special prayers to take you into heaven?" Was that our responsibility, the family of the dead? Every time me and the family visited, we all went to church together over my dad's last ten years. We were good Catholics. We have our faith. We believe in God, purgatory, and heaven. Everything is just blind faith. There is no proof of any of it. It's just faith in the word of God.

I went to bed the night after the drive home. I was thinking about dad and saying prayers for him and my family. I wondered over and over, what really is life all about? I already missed my father bad. That night in bed I asked if dad was safe. This time I asked for guidance. "Answer me in a way I cannot misunderstand. I am desperate to know if dad is safe."

I don't know how long I laid in my bed before I fell asleep. My wife was sound asleep next to me, and the kids

were asleep in their bedrooms like every other night. I did all
I could to not cry that day. I hurt. I had a big hole in my heart.
When it sunk in that my dad was gone forever, I called on my
Catholic faith and my Ojibwe roots. Dad and I had gotten
very close over his last ten years. We did a lot of things
together. We talked about everything. But I guess we did not
talk about death. I wish we had, but it's an uncomfortable
topic for just about everyone. I would have liked to know
what my dad thought about death and heaven and all.

Suddenly, I was awakened from my sleep by a hot,
burning heat on my left shoulder. I opened my eyes and
could not believe what I saw. A small, foggy, and sparkling
light floated around the bedroom. It was about the size of a
golf ball. I sat up in bed and just watched it for a few seconds.
I blinked several times to make sure my eyes were not
playing tricks on me. But, sure enough, it was real. I was not
seeing things. I was wide awake when the small, glowing orb
stopped moving around and came to me. It just floated there,
about an arm's length from my nose. "What are you? Why
are you here," I wondered?

Like my eagle on Highway 55 in '92, the orb was
important. For a few seconds I forgot to breathe. My heart
was beating in my throat. I swallowed hard not knowing
really what to do. Then it spoke! The words were crisp, clear,
and gentle. It was dad. He spoke to me with the calm
strength I remembered as a kid but had not heard since the
Deer Stand Murders. Dad said nine words I will never forget.
He said, "I am okay, Scotty. Do not worry about me."

The orb stayed in my bedroom for a total of ten seconds.

It was long enough for me to know it was real. I not only heard dad's voice, but I also felt his presence. I felt shrouded in a familiar warmth—my father's love. The orb floated at an arm's length from me for just a few seconds. Then it zipped out the window, the upper right corner.

Like my other unexplainable experiences, my first reaction was to think it could not have happened. The orb left the bedroom. It zipped out the upper righthand corner. Then my wife sat up in bed. She could see I was not myself. She asked if I was all right. I think I told her my dad had just spoke to me. I was still reacting to the whole thing. I decided to go sleep on the sofa. Maybe there I could sort things out. I knew it happened. After all the eagle encounters around dad's funeral, and all the things that had happened to me, I decided not to go into detail on the orb.

My friends and family members want to believe me when I talk about my unusual experiences, like my eagle encounters. I know it is hard. It's even hard for me, and I've seen these things with my own two eyes. They know I will never lie, but they will think maybe I'm mistaken. Maybe my mind is playing tricks on me?

I've learned to take my time to process these things. I needed the alone time to sort things out. Then for a long time I was reluctant to talk about any of it. I eventually reached a point in my life where I didn't care who believed me. My focus had moved. My priorities moved from trying so hard to get people to believe me to trying to understand exactly what happened and why. People have different levels of tolerance when it comes to the unknown. Some will never get there. Others get it but must move at their own speed. Nothing I say or do changes that. By April 2005, I had accepted the fact unexplainable spiritual events were going to be a routine part of my life. I saw the orb. My dad spoke to me, and then it left my bedroom. I have no idea why I was chosen for this experience. But I want to understand one day.

The morning after the orb in our bedroom, I was still not quite ready to talk. It was my first orb. And I still got some cold chills thinking about it and my father's words. I did talk to my wife briefly about it, but I downplayed the whole thing. I didn't have any physical proof. The place on my shoulder where I felt a hot burning sensation had no marks, no indication that I was actually burned even though it woke me up and I felt it.

My orb was white. I did some research and found there are ten major categories of color, and there are a lot of subcategories that takes the count up to thirty-four. It is clear there are a lot of very specific variations people observe and science cannot explain. For those who believe the orb phenomenon is spiritual, each color has a meaning. I find it interesting that the color defines the nature and mission of the visiting orb.

Pink orbs are about compassion and affection. Red are high energy and restlessness. Orange orbs are about healing and motivational spirits of good fortune. There are blue, green, and purple orbs with special purposes. The least favorable orbs are browns and blacks. They are connected to earth. They are insecure, tortured, trapped, and they are believed to be unhappy spirits stuck in the earth plane.

A white orb visited me in Minnetrista. White and silver orbs are said to be pure energy high-frequency orbs of strength and new power. That would fit my father; he was a new spirit at the time. I read a white orb is a visiting spirit that brings peace, harmony, and love. I think the orb touched my shoulder to wake me up. That would explain the hot burning sensation. There were no burn marks, so I will never know for sure. Right after my father spoke to me the orb left the bedroom. It went out the upper right side of the closed window.

The Native American Indians have spoken of orbs and sacred burial mounds for many centuries. I just happen to have some protected Indian burial mounds by my Minnetrista house. They say they are powerful, spiritual sites —portals into the afterlife. I believe the site by my house may be connected to my orb and dreams. Burial mounds are built by the Indians in very specific locations. Maybe I am some kind of a receptacle sensitive to these powers.

A year after the orb came to me, I took the family to Milwaukee to celebrate Grandma Kathleen's ninetieth birthday. There, I met a Catholic priest, Father Bill. Although I only have been with him twice in my life (Grandma's birthday and her funeral), I felt very comfortable talking to him. He knew Grandma and Grandpa for decades. Although Father Bill visited parishioners on occasion, he visited Grandma Kathleen and Grandpa Larry most holidays and often special family occasions.

At Grandma Kathleen's ninetieth birthday celebration, I had the opportunity to talk to Father Bill privately. I told him about my dream of dad's death before it happened. And I told him about the orb that visited me after my dad's funeral. As I stumbled through the events unsure of how the priest took it, I was surprised he listened intently and did not appear shocked by what I was saying. When I finished, he started on my dream first. Father Bill said, with the devout clarity of a lifelong clergyman, "God sometimes prepares us for a death. God knows who among us needs"—what Father Bill described as—"a little help." That meant a lot to me.

When it came to the orb, he just smiled. But not in a funny way. It was more a smile of experience and reassurance. Father Bill was not at all surprised by the orb. He said several members of the church had come to him over the years with their orb encounters. He said it has happened ten or twelve times over his life as a priest. In all cases, they seek answers and some reassurance they are not crazy. Father Bill admitted he didn't know much about orbs, although there is a lot written about them. He did believe they exist and are a gift from God. The orb is a visiting spirit of one who passed. In my case, he told me it seemed clear my father came to help me with the grieving process. He added it was a good thing, but we might never understand more than that in this life. But I needed to know more about the sacred Indian mounds next to my house. I feel certain they have something to do with my spiritual experiences.

19

> "We only occupy a physical body during this lifetime. Our creator puts a person on earth with a purpose. Once that purpose is fulfilled our physical body dies and our spirt passes on into the afterlife."
> —Ojibwe Indian Nation belief

April 2005—Minnetrista, Minnesota

The land is spiritually charged, and I'm a lightning rod. What could possibly go wrong? We built our house in Minnetrista in 1999, on the edge of a residential development on Lake Minnetonka. We were the last house on a dead-end road, Lakeside Circle. We really liked the view—rolling hills, pristine fields, and thick woodlands as far as the eye could see.

They said the land would never be developed. The
rolling fields and towering trees went about a mile west to
the Dakota Rail Regional Trail and north to the Westonka
Regional Park. We thought building on the last lot on
Lakeside Circle would be perfect. We would always have a
great view and our privacy. I remember they said there are
some Indian mounds out there. That was the reason the land
was protected and would never be developed.

If you Google search Minnetrista, Minnesota, you will
find Indian mounds are prevalent in the area. They are such
a big part of the Hennepin County landscape that our
neighboring town of 10,000 people is named Mound.

There are a lot of theories about the builders and
purposes. Mounds come in all shapes and sizes—small to
enormous, round, horseshoe shaped, square, rectangular,
and more. Most are spiritually charged. I believe the mounds
by my house in Minnetrista may have had something to do
with my unusual experiences—bizarre dreams, the orb,
shadow visitors in the night, some of my eagle encounters,
and the owls.

The first mounds were built by prehistoric American
Indians. The Elizabeth Mounds in Illinois date back to 4,000
BC. Like the Mayans, who built temples on Yucatan
Peninsula, they built enormous mounds all over the Great
Lakes area and in the Mississippi River Valley down to the
Gulf of Mexico. All these earthworks required movement of
thousands of tons of dirt, clay, and rock. Archeologists
believe it was almost an impossible task because they were
physically limited. They had not yet harnessed beasts of

burden, nor did they know about the wheel that long ago.
They were all hunters, fishers, and gatherers. Like the
Egyptians who used slave labor to build pyramids over
decades, it is likely the Mayans and prehistoric Indians did
the same. However they did it, the fact remains they built
pyramids and mounds.

Some mounds also had to be built as recent as the 1400s,
the century when the Euro-American settlers started to
arrive. Because the Ojibwe and Dakota Indians are the third
and fourth largest Indian nations, I believe Ojibwe elders
when they tell me some of the mounds were built by their
forefathers many moons ago.

Although mounds have different religious and cultural
purposes, most are known to be sacred burial grounds.
Through advanced detection technology we know there are
thousands of human-remains interred in many of them.
They are protected by city, county, state, and federal
governments. Some mounds are closed to the public out of
traditions and respect for the dead. Many mounds are open
to the public. It provides a great opportunity for education
on the history and spirituality of the Native American
Indians.

I call them private mounds. An old Indian cemetery
swallowed by the woods. They are protected like all other
mounds. They are often unmarked, unpromoted, and
unknown to people outside the area. These are the mounds
by my Minnetrista home. They are in the woods and not
fenced off. People can take walks in the fields and woods and
visit them. But like any other cemetery they cannot disturb

them in any way. They may be overgrown but they need to be respected, people are buried there. Some of the mounds are obvious. Others are lost in the rolling terrain and overgrowth. And some are cared for by the living generations.

When we lived in Minnetrista from 1999 to 2012, I was very busy working for Conwood. I sold tobacco products in parts of Minnesota, the Dakotas, and Wisconsin. I always made it a point to visit the Indian reservations throughout the Midwest. In my travels, I learned mounds are connected to large clans (kin groups and lineages). There are mounds built twenty feet high and 900 feet long. Some of the burial mounds can reach even sixty feet in height.

Native American Indians built flat-topped pyramids with big earthen enclosures. In Tennessee, there is a four-sided, flat-topped mound believed to have been used as an elevated stage for religious-ritual performances. In Ohio, they built mounds in circles, squares, and octagons with hundreds of enclosed sections for burials. Archeologists have found large tombs beneath massive mounds crowded with bodies and funerary objects. The largest mound is Monks Mound. Its base covers five-hundred acres and it rises a hundred feet above the Mississippi River flood plain. It is close to the size of the Great Pyramid of Giza.

The Indian mounds by my house are small. They are not a destination spot on maps or in tourist guides. They are on fifty-acre Sioux Indian burial grounds. Many hundreds of years ago, the Sioux Indians chose this location for a reason. Although contents of a mound are important, so are location and design. The spirituality emanating from these burial grounds next to my house must be more intense than all the other places I go. I believe these mounds have had something to do with my unusual experiences—dreams, visions, and more.

Like the giant stone heads on Easter Island, and the Pyramids in Egypt, and the Mayan Temples on the other side of the world—Yucatan Peninsula—location means something. We know there are astronomical connections, but there are more. We do not know why the Sioux Indians selected these particular fifty acres for sacred burial grounds. I do not know how or why I ended up living next to them. But I do know there are reasons. I know everything matters. Because the Native American Indians are a people most connected to Mother Earth, and because their preparations for departing from this world to the afterlife is a big deal, the place from where they depart must be special. What do the Sioux Indians know about this land now called Minnetrista? How powerful is the spirituality there? Out of all the other places in the world I could be, why did I move to Minnetrista and live by these Indian mounds?

In April 2005, the month after my father's burial services, the shimmering white orb came through my window. It entered my bedroom and burned me, and my father spoke to me! Did the sacred Sioux burial grounds outside my window have anything to do with that?

On the days of March 7, 2005, 2006, and 2007, an eagle came to me and sat in my tree. March 7, 2005 is the day my father died. Did the sacred Sioux burial grounds outside my window have anything to do with that?

The owls—those foreboding deliverers of bad news—sat on my roof just weeks before the unexpected death of my close friend and family member. Did the sacred Sioux burial grounds outside my window have anything to do with that?

My dreams, me climbing to perilous heights and dropping into a giant eagle nest of broken branches bathed in blood; and me reaching for the eagle feather as baby eaglets peck at my arms and the mother eagle approaches from above, her massive wings spread and razor-sharp talons closing in on me. Did the sacred Sioux burial grounds outside my window have anything to do with that?

I may never know that about my mystifying experiences. Some think there is a gateway. Souls of the dead leave this world and pass through it into the afterlife. Is it possible this gateway (portal) allows spirits to enter this world from the afterlife? Is that why my father was able to visit me in Minnetrista? Do eagles and owls see and hear these spirits come and go? Is it possible I am some kind of a lightning rod in this world that gives me eyes and ears to experience these spirits?

20

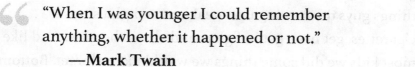

> "When I was younger I could remember anything, whether it happened or not."
> —Mark Twain

June 2005—Rice Lake, Wisconsin

We were always close. Greg was born exactly two years to the day after me, September 13, 1963. Like me, he came into this world at Deaconess Hospital in Milwaukee. Deaconess no longer exists today. Neola and Dennis split up three years after Greg was born.

Looking back, I think we always had a solid connection. The world could change but we always knew we would be there for each other. Although people get divorces all the time, that kind of a change does have an impact on kids.

Especially young kids that don't understand a lot of things. Greg was three and I was five, when all of a sudden, our world spun out of control. In an instant we did not have a mother and we moved our life to another house. I do not remember if we were told much more than "your mother and I have decided to go our own ways". What does that even mean to a five-year-old?

I could always talk to Greg. I think he looked up to me as a big brother. He knew Scotty would watch out for him, take care of him no matter what. Greg will tell you today we did some really crazy things growing up. He often said it would make a great movie, better than the *Godfather*. Somehow, we got through things without any major setbacks. We did the things guys do growing up: sneak out at night, smoke cigarettes, get beer, get in fights, and chase the girls. And like most kids we did some things we would like to forget. Bottom line, the Roux brothers are tight still today.

I left Wisconsin, stayed single a long time, and went the coat-and-tie salesman route. Greg followed in our father's footsteps. He stayed in Wisconsin, got married, had a family, joined a union, and went the carpentry route. Although we both worked hard all our lives, Greg worked physically harder all his life and that tends to put a lot of wear-and-tear on the body. Like dad, Greg had some heart issues later in life. But unlike dad, he listens pretty much to doctors and takes his meds most of the time. But I don't think he ever slowed down.

On November 22, 2004, Greg learned about the Deer Stand Shootings on a TV monitor at Disney World. That year both Greg and I did not go on the deer drive at Rice Lake. I had my commitments in Minnetrista—work and my annual poker game at my house—and Greg took his family on a vacation. They drove to Orlando, Florida. Greg told me he went into shock when he saw the first news reports on the shootings at Rice Lake. He knew dad was there.

The national news coverage was on every TV channel. In the beginning, they did not know what was going on. The lead headlines were that someone is shooting Wisconsin deer hunters in the Blue Hills east of Rice Lake. The news did not release names of the dead or injured right away—standard procedure to give police time to notify next of kin. They do not like family members to learn of a death on TV.

The trouble was Greg knew dad and our distant cousins and our hunting buddies hunt exactly where the nightmare was unfolding.

Dad called me. He was shaken up and not comfortable talking on the phone while this catastrophic mess continued to unfold around him. I don't think he was up to making too many phone calls. He didn't tell me much because he didn't know much at the time. The investigation was still underway. The arrival of the police and removal of the injured and the dead from the woods was a work in progress. Dad called Francine. She was on her way to Rice Lake. I didn't ask who else Dad and Francine called. It just didn't come to mind. I was in shock too.

Greg pulled his family out of Disney World, and they started driving back to Wisconsin on the same day. He tried to get Francine but was unable. She was en route to Rice

Lake. Her focus was on dad. I know she worried about him a lot and her own safety. I know after I talked to dad for just a few minutes he was not himself. He was living in the single greatest trauma of his life. Meanwhile, Greg is driving from Orlando to Milwaukee listening to the radio and catching the news at gas stations each time he stops for gas.

Greg finally got a hold of Francine. Needless to say, he was a bit angry she did not call him earlier. And it did not help he had to drive twelve-hundred miles with a worried family not knowing dad's condition or the status of distant cousins and hunting friends. Over the years, Greg had deer hunted with most of the Rice Lake hunters one time or another. When you hunt with people there is a lot of quality down time in the wilderness. Over the years you can get close to each other, great friends. And you know their families. Most non-hunters don't appreciate hunters' time with each other before and after the hunt is just as important as the actual hunt itself. Hunters share a common love for the outdoors, respect for the animals they hunt, and good old-fashioned comradery. And the sport is not limited to men.

Driving back home, Greg had a lot of windshield time. He used it to sort through all the news reports in his attempt to figure out what actually happened, who was really hurt, and who could possibly be dead. As usual with big stories the news media sensationalizes everything. The information is incomplete and often wrong. It seems they have only one priority—being first. Being accurate is a distant two. Unfortunately, Greg had to navigate through the barrage of news snippets to reconstruct a horrific reality for seventeen hours. When he finally connected with Francine he was not in the best of moods.

First, he wanted to know if dad was all right. Second, he wanted to know why she did not call him. He did not enjoy his trip from Disneyworld through hell. Francine's first five words pretty much shut Greg down. Everything he felt before this call did not matter. Francine waited for Greg to stop talking. Then she said, "I lost your dad today!"

Greg knew dad had not been shot. By then he knew dad was a hero. He jumped into the back of a pickup truck and rode into the belly of the beast not knowing who was shooting, where they were shooting, or why they were shooting. Dad was only capable of one goal at that moment. Get as many people as he could out of there. When Francine said she lost dad that day, Greg knew exactly what she meant. He had not been shot, but he was not the man we all knew. Not anymore.

When Greg finally got home and got to dad, he understood even more. Greg looked into dad's eyes and saw what he had seen twenty-six years ago. Dad's eyes were foggy and empty. It was like no one was home, even though dad was standing there, his heart was beating, he was breathing, and he was responsive, although now a man of few words. When Greg embraced dad, he felt a slight tremble. Dad could not hide his fear—it was still there. But the family did not talk about it. We did not talk much about that day. Not for a while. It was hard for everyone.

When Greg was fifteen he and dad decided to go hunting.

They took dad's jeep and headed out for Rice Lake that evening. It was Wisconsin cold, and the snow had been coming down all day. Maybe it would let up or maybe they would drive out of it. But none of that happened. As they left the city the cars dwindled, and the snowfall increased. It was a white wonderland, and their headlights were alone. People were just not out in this mess. They were having second thoughts about the hunting trip. The weather was getting worse. Should they turn around and go back home? By decision time they were closer to Rice Lake than home. They stayed the course even though they could be the only ones out that night.

They were down to a single pair of tire-ruts in the deep snow. And they ran down the center of the two-lane road. The snow was deep, maybe a foot. They had reached the point when venturing outside the ruts would be very dangerous. It could send the Jeep off into a ditch or worse. There were a lot of ravines and bridges and fat trees. They did not want to run into any one of them. And even if they survived, they would be stranded in subzero temperatures.

Then it happened. Another first pair of headlights appeared straight ahead, and they were coming fast. On a normal night it would be no big deal; the approaching car would simply pass by on their left side. But on this night, there was only one set of tire-ruts in the center of the road cutting through more than a foot of snow. The lights that came toward the Jeep were bigger and sat higher—it was not a car. It was a semi-truck barreling down the hill. And now they could see it was out of control. It was locked into the ruts the Jeep clung to.

Greg said dad froze! His eyes were locked straight ahead, and his hands squeezed the steering wheel. As the truck got closer Greg yelled to dad—you gotta move over! The truck was not leaving the ruts. As it slid down the hill with wheels locked, Greg could see the steel and ice coming to them was not controlled by the driver. It was a giant sled shooting down the hill.

As it got closer dad did nothing. The truck was seconds away from crushing the Jeep head-on. Greg pulled the steering wheel hard. The Jeep jumped out of the ruts and spun off the road as the semi skidded by, locked in the deep ruts. A ton of ice and snow buried half the Jeep on the left side of the road, but they were alive. In silence, Greg watched the red taillights in the side mirror as the semi pulled out of its jackknife and started to gain control at the bottom of the hill. Then the red lights disappeared on the last turn. Greg knew then there was no way that truck could have moved out of the ruts. And dad did nothing.

When Greg looked over, dad was still holding the steering wheel and looking straight ahead. Greg yelled at him, asking if he was okay and if he knew they were almost killed. When dad turned to him, Greg saw the look he would see twenty-six years later—the frozen and foggy eyes, and the empty stare. Dad had to escape the danger. He went to his safe place.

Dad muttered to Greg he did a good thing. Dad gave Greg all the credit that one time. Dad did not know he had checked out. He did not know he locked up. It was as if he left the Jeep and returned after the incident. Jeff, the hunter, said dad did not know if they should go back home or continue on to Rice Lake. Jeff was the one who made the decision for dad. They were going hunting—they were closer to Rice Lake than home. He knew dad needed to lie down as soon as possible. And they could use the quiet, quality time together after what they had been through.

Greg knew when dad was ready to drive out of the ditch, too. Greg is a smoker. At age fifteen he had to sneak. After the near-miss he needed a smoke, bad. Greg got up the nerve to ask dad if he could light up a cigarette. Dad's eyes changed. He emerged from the moment and yelled there was no way Greg was going to smoke up the car. Then dad started the jeep, pulled out of the ditch, found the ruts, and they went on to Rice Lake. Greg thought it was odd that dad acted like nothing had happened the rest of the trip. It was the only way he could handle it.

Looking back over the years, dad was not one for scary things. He avoided thrillers and horror shows. He had to leave the room when we were watching *The Exorcist*. And dad never handled bad news well. He was a gentle, good-hearted, fun-loving man by nature. The trauma of the Deer Stand Shootings had to be the single greatest disaster of his life. Both Greg and I knew dad was unable to handle the terror of it all. He went to his safe place. Francine, Greg, and I all saw it in his eyes. This time he would not come out.

Two years after the Rice Lake shootings a new park opened. It honored the six hunters who died on that terrible day in 2004: Robert Crotteau, age forty-two; Joey Crotteau, age twenty; Al Laski, age forty-three; Mark Roidt, age twenty-eight; Jessica Willers, age twenty-seven; Dennis Drew, age fifty-five. The memorial sits at the entrance of Hunters Memorial Park. The tribute inscribed on the lighted granite sign reads, "Gone, but not forgotten." Although my father's name does not appear on the list of the dead, the words on that memorial speak to our family and many other families. There were many people wounded that day, most without bullets. They walked away with their invisible wounds. Some died from these wounds just months later. Others died years later. All are victims of that infamous day, November 21, 2004.

On the back of the memorial's engraved granite is another important message. It captures the hearts of the hunters. "They loved God, family, and country." The words set the perfect tone for this new park in Rice Lake, Wisconsin.

"This park is a gathering place for picnicking, playing, and reflecting. It represents what the hunters care most about—family, friends, and enjoying the outdoors."

Greg's experience in the Jeep with dad years ago is one of many memories we have from growing up in Milwaukee and hunting in the Blue Hills near Rice Lake. Greg and I spent a lot of time together trying to figure out life, like every other kid growing up in the turbulent sixties and seventies. Looking back, I am reminded of other memories as adults. We have spent a lot of time together as working and family men with busy lives and responsibilities. Just like kids, we could talk to each other about anything. And we had a lot of opportunities. We always found time to get together for hunting and the holidays.

After the orb visited me in April, I decided to keep it to myself. I guess I was worried no one would believe me anyway. In the beginning, I didn't even believe me, and I saw it with my own two eyes. I knew I was going to see Greg in June of 2005 at Rice Lake, so I started to think about telling him. I know he would listen and not judge. And he would not question whether I saw it or not. He knows I have been having a lot of odd and unexplainable experiences lately. Greg might think I am a little crazy, but he would believe me, and that helps. Maybe he could have some helpful thoughts for me. I also knew talking out loud about it could help some.

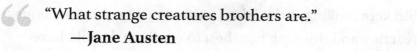

21

> "What strange creatures brothers are."
> —Jane Austen

May 2005—Rice Lake, Wisconsin

Truth be told, deep down, I did not want to talk to anybody about the white orb. That night in my bedroom at my Minnetrista home, I was not sure how to process what happened over the course of ten seconds. I do remember pinching myself hard to make sure I was not dreaming. I did not talk about it after my very brief comments to my wife that night. I let the whole experience die a silent death. I learned avoidance is a convenient way to handle a lot of difficult things in life.

Six weeks later, I took a trip to Rice Lake. It was almost three months after we buried dad. On the road (windshield time), I made my decision. I would tell Greg about the orb. He knew me well. It would not take him long to pick up that I had something on my mind. Rather than deny it and dance around it, I decided to get him aside as soon as possible after my arrival. I would disguise the alone-time as one of our brotherly, mano a mano moments. I never felt like I had to tell Greg about the orb. But as I drove to Rice Lake, I realized I did want him to know about it. I think it was a brother thing.

We went off alone on the back deck. Greg sat on the steps with his back to me. He was looking at Minnow Lake. I jumped right into it. I said, "Dad came into my bedroom a few weeks ago. He came in the form of a white orb!"

I know my opening line shook him a lot. He stiffened up but kept looking at the lake. I paused maybe thirty seconds reacting and thinking how best to continue. I could have worked up to it, but it was late now. I did need to smooth things over a little before I went further. I said, "It's okay to be scared, Greg. I was too at first."

After another short silence he asked his one question. "How did you know it was dad?"

It was the right question. He didn't ask about the orb or if I was sure about what happened. He was already past that— a good sign. But I think my next words shook him even more than my opening line. I told him dad spoke to me in his own calm voice. Dad had said that I didn't need to worry about him anymore. He was safe.

Still looking at Minnow Lake, Greg whispered, "I know you were worried about him, Scottie. That's the kind of guy you are." He could not have said anything else that would have helped me more than those words. They were perfect.

Greg jumped to his feet and pointed. I will not use his exact words, but they were along the lines of "Holy cow feces!"

I followed his finger to a big bald eagle. It had to be an eight-foot wing span. There it was coming right to us. With eyes wide and hearts beating in our ears, we watched the muscular legs extend and talons open. It approached the top of the tallest tree and slowed. It flapped its massive wings, settled down onto a fat limb, and folded its wings to its sides. This eagle stared at Greg. This was his eagle. I smiled inside. This was the perfect moment.

The eagle's eyes stayed on Greg. Then it turned its head to the east horizon and jumped off the tree. We watched it glide over Minnow Lake and disappear into the woods. I will not forget Greg's face, when he turned to me. The eagle cemented our moment in time.

He lit a cigarette. His hand trembled. He smiled and said, "You are a freak, big brother!" We laughed. It felt good. My unexplainable load felt lighter—the eagles, the owls, the dreams, and now the orb. Greg is with me. My decision to tell him was the right one.

It further confirmed my feelings about life and afterlife. We know very little. We have our religion but there is not much information other than when we die our souls go to a good place (heaven) if we are good, or a bad place (hell) if we are bad. Theologians and philosophers share theories on what life is all about, but the bottom line is we should be good to each other and serve God—that I know for sure.

What about relationships with loved ones? How important is that? And what about relationships with all those people we spend our life with? Are they important? We give them a lot of our time. They are a big part of our growth and development as a human being. If they are important in the grand scheme of things, it would seem logical that after death our souls would be able to return to this life and take care of unfinished business with these important people who shaped us and whom we shaped. If not, how important could any relationship be left unfinished?

Are there portals into the afterlife, gateways to other dimensions? If they exist, it seems logical that passage both ways would be possible. I wonder, do the Native American Indians know where portals are? Is that where they put their burial-grounds? It seems so because Native American Indians have a lot to say about the afterlife and spirits visiting this world. Their rituals and ceremonies have been passed down for thousands of years. Portals in burial grounds makes perfect sense!

That day at Rice Lake, after Greg and I left the back deck, we did not talk about portals, eagles, or orbs again. It would take me a long while to get comfortable with the orb experience. Unlike eagles that are a part of my everyday life, the orb was ten seconds. Will there be more?

When I told Greg everything, he did not say a word. He smiled at me like always. Greg did not need proof. He knows I do not lie nor am I easily fooled. Although, we have never talked about my hidden fears, I think he knows I have them. After the eagle experience that day, his eyes were wide open. I know he has his hidden fears, too. Greg also knows that I did not invite any of this into my life. I have always been the level-headed one in the family. I think he knew all of this was happening to me. I wasn't making anything happen.

Greg is always with me because we are brothers, and because he has his own set of unexplainable experiences. And because we are half Ojibwe Indian. That means we recognize and respect the spirit world.

22

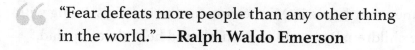

"Fear defeats more people than any other thing in the world." —**Ralph Waldo Emerson**

December 2004—Minneapolis, Wisconsin

I am reminded of the day after the shootings in 2004. The Green Bay Packers had a scheduled game to play the St. Louis Rams at Lambeau Field—Monday night football. But the whole state of Wisconsin, and a lot of people across the country, were still in shock over the terrible tragedy in the woods by Rice Lake. That Monday night more than 65,000 fans attended the Packers-Rams game. My heart skipped a beat—almost everyone there wore hunter orange in tribute to the victims of the Deer Stand Murders. There was also a moment of silence shared by the country. It was a special time for a short prayer and reflection—another cherished memory.

That year and into most of 2005 there were tribute banquets and auctions and fundraisers across the state. Money raised helped pay some medical bills for the wounded survivors and the funeral expenses for the victims. Most of the money raised financed the development of Hunters Memorial Park in Rice Lake.

The aftermath of the shootings was hard for a lot of people, especially the survivors and the families of the lost. I would soon discover the experience for my father was insurmountable. Christmas 2004 was a month after the tragedy. We thought it would be good for dad and Frannie to come to my home in Minnetrista for the holidays. Being with the children, Ryan and Kaitlyn, should help cheer up dad, take his mind off his worries. He really loved his role as grandpa.

To my surprise, Christmas 2004 would be when I began to realize dad was not getting past the tragedy. It was a month after that terrible event, I did not expect dad to be a 100 percent. However, I did expect him to be on the mend. He was not. He was getting worse.

I had picked up some great tickets to the Packers-Vikings game scheduled that Christmas Eve. I would take dad and a close family friend, one who dad really liked. Packy really liked my dad. Packy was almost like a member of the family. What a great guy this Packy was to everyone and to my dad over the years. I thought it was a good time for Packy to see dad. The tragedy was in the past. We needed to move on.

Packy really surprised me on the night of the football game. He brought my dad a nice Christmas present—a beautiful pair of fireplace gloves. I was happy Packy did that. What a great guy. Dad seemed happy to see Packy, and he seemed to really like his gift. But something was not right. Something was off. Dad was just not himself. He wasn't kidding around. He just didn't act like he usually did. Dad was a jokester. All the time kidding around. But not this time.

I thought the three of us were going to have one great time together at the Metrodome in downtown Minneapolis on Christmas Eve. I thought Packer's football was the best medicine for just about everything. That night it was below freezing outside, there was some snow on the ground, and the Christmas decorations were all over the city. It was great Packer football weather if we were playing outside at Lambeau Field. It was still fun even though we were sitting inside the Minnesota Vikings Metrodome. We had some of the best seats in the stadium, too. I got the tickets from a friend.

The Christmas Eve football game turned out to be one of the best Packer games ever. It was high scoring. There were a lot of great football plays. And our Packers pulled out a win in fourth quarter—Green Bay, thirty-four, and Minnesota, thirty-one. I could not have asked for a better football game to cheer up my dad. But his mind was still on November 21, 2004.

Dad was just not with us. He was not himself. He always loved Packer games, but not that night. He was quiet and detached. He sat in the chair next to me, but he was somewhere else. He had little interest in the game or the moment—he seemed distracted. His reactions to Packer touchdowns and great plays were not him. That night dad would only reply to questions. He did not start a single conversation.

I realized that night he was not getting past the tragedy. Packy and I tried to get him to relax and have some fun, but he was just not having it. The best way I can describe him that night at the Packer game is to say he acted like a long-distant runner after a grueling race. He was somewhere between exhausted and broken. Even on Christmas Day dad was not himself. He went through the motions with the kids, but he was not the same. I did not say anything about it to him or Frannie. I didn't want to make him more uncomfortable. I didn't want to stir things up. It was clear to me dad was not getting better.

He said he wanted to plan a big New Year's Eve party at his house in Rice Lake. He wanted the whole family there. He must have asked me five times to be sure to get everyone there. I could feel the desperation. I knew something was off.

Dad would die nine weeks later.

I wonder if the big New Year's Eve party was about him seeing everyone for one last time. I felt like he wanted to say goodbye. I also wonder if he went to Jamaica to die. I know it's a terrible thing to think, but the Deer Stand Murders hurt my father so deeply that I don't think he was ever coming back. That terrible tragedy broke his heart in a way he could not fix.

Frannie told me dad had nightmares ever since the shootings. She said he would wake up most nights scared to death. He kept reliving that day. When he went in to help those wounded, he had to trust God would protect him. Even with that strong faith, the shots were popping all around him and bullets were flying. I know he was waiting for one to find him. But he kept going. Then he got the wounded and the dying in the back of the pickup truck and they snaked out of the woods to safety. Dad prayed and kept pressure on bleeding stomach wounds. Months later. Dad was losing touch with reality. His imagination was going wild. Nothing is resolved. The trial would not take place for two years. Dad would wake up at night afraid they were coming for him next. The memories of the wounded and the dead tormented him until he died. He never got over the blood on his hands and the loss of friends. Death was the only way to find peace.

23

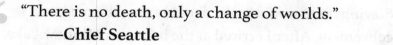

> "There is no death, only a change of worlds."
> —Chief Seattle

November 2006—Rice Lake, Wisconsin

I bought the Rice Lake house from Frannie in June 2006, a year after dad died. We loved the place and Frannie wanted to move and find work; she needed to start a new life on her own. I knew the money from the sale of the house would help with her transition. Although I did not know it at the time, I would move the family to Rice Lake six years later.

Frannie moved and worked for a metal finishing business, in Wausau. Later she would do custodial work at a junior high school in the area and then eventually return to Milwaukee. Frannie has always been a roll-up-the-sleeves person. She was very involved in raising her three boys. Then, she was back to taking care of herself like she did for many years before marrying dad. Frannie is a very special lady with gypsy in her blood. Today, she will tell you it never left. She's still looking for her next destination. Frannie has always been a big part of my life. I blame her for my success. She was a great mother when I needed one, and she is a real friend. I can always count on her being there for me, just like I will always be there for her. I know losing dad has not been easy for her, but I also know Frannie is a survivor and a positive-thinking person that loves life.

The night before the 2006 opening day of deer season, I went up to the Rice Lake house alone to spend the night. Staying there would make deer hunting the next day convenient. After I arrived at the house on Minnow Lake, I got all my hunting gear ready for the deer drive the next morning. I ate dinner, watched some TV, and decided to go to bed early. 4:30 AM would come fast. I needed to be rested and alert. Deer drives always start early and everyone has a job to do. We count on each other to be on time and to do our parts. One mess up, everyone pays the price.

Life in Rice Lake is easy. The small town is laid back and the countryside magnificent. I loved the house Dad built. I always felt at home and I always felt safe with the family. I even felt safe when I was there alone. The night before that 2006 deer drive was cold. There was a crescent moon and a cloudless sky. I felt good; all organized, well fed, and ready to hit the sack. I had no problem falling asleep—then something happened that would change everything.

I awoke in the middle of the night to a sharp jab in my lower back. It hurt so much I actually jumped. It felt like a pointed stick, or a spear, poking me. I even reached under the covers for the area expecting blood. When I found the spot, it was sore, not wet. I was not mortally wounded. Maybe it was just a weird cramp. But I had never had a cramp in that spot before.

When I opened my eyes a little, I could not believe what I saw. The soft light from the sliver-moon fell through the windows and filled the room. There was enough light to make out everything. I knew I was in my Rice Lake bedroom. I knew I was not dreaming. I was very wide awake rubbing my sore spot. I saw shadows move. I froze. They were moving around my bed. I squinted so they would think I was still asleep. I would fake it until I figured out what was happening. I watched the line of shadow figures slowly move around the bed without a sound.

I could tell right away they were not looking at me. Their heads faced the person in front of them. Or they could be just looking forward or be blind and holding onto the one in front of them. I opened my eyes more and blinked to make sure I was not converting a chair or bed post into shadow people. But the figures were moving. Chairs and bed posts don't move.

I stopped counting at six—there were a lot. They were tall and short and built like males. They seemed to dance in the circle around my bed. I could only see the sides and end of the bed. Since the headboard is against the wall, I knew they would have to go in and out of the wall. Some heads were bowed for a while and others looked up for a while. Some arms reached for the ceiling, and some reached for the floor. They seemed to take turns bowing and reaching up. And they kept a slow, steady pace. I did not hear feet shuffle or breathing or chants. There was no music or drums beating, but the shadow figures moved to a synchronized rhythm.

The moonlight was bright enough to see the shadow people but too weak to make out faces or clothes and to see if they were holding onto anything like a stick or spear or knife or saber to jab me. I never felt fear. I felt curiosity. For some reason, I never felt I was in danger. Instead, I needed to understand what was going on. I had never seen anything like it in my life. As I laid in bed, I wanted to know who the shadow people were and, more than anything, what were they doing in my bedroom.

I wondered if they were actual people or spirits. After a while, I concluded they were spirits because they were going in and out of walls and made no sounds. I could not see their feet, but it seemed as if they were floating. I watched them for about a full minute. Then something new happened. Lighted symbols and lighted letters appeared on the walls at the ceiling and flowed down all four walls. They flowed down like an unending waterfall. Each lighted letter or symbol or sign was the size of my opened hand.

They flowed slow and continuous like scrolling for reading purposes. It was like the lines of a script with letters and symbols in a different language. They continued to flow down the walls from the ceiling and disappeared into the floor. There were hundreds of different signs and symbols. I did not recognize any. They flowed behind the shadow people uninterrupted for about five minutes. It was long enough for me to be sure of what was happening. I was wide awake.

I did not see the shadow people come into my room, but I did see the beginning of the symbol flow. After five minutes of flowing, everything started to fade. The symbols faded away first, and then the shadow people faded away. The room remained quiet but was not empty. Everything returned to normal, the furniture, me, and the moonlight. I checked the clock. It was 3:30 in the morning. I turned on a lamp by the bed. The place looked like I had left it when I went to bed. Nothing disturbed. No residues. No marks. Nothing moved or out of order. The only thing I could find that was not there before was the mark on my lower back. And it still hurt.

I would not be going back to bed that night. I could not possibly sleep. And I had to get up in an hour anyway. I just sat there. I felt exactly like I did after the orb zipped out of my bedroom window in Minnetrista and out of my life. I was alone, in awe, and confused. What just happened to me? What is this one about? I looked up and said, "Lord, I don't know what's going on with me or around me, but could you please help me understand it one day?"

Yes, I did see it. Yes, it lasted for about six minutes. No, there is no proof anything happened that night at Rice Lake. I believe it had something to do with my Ojibwe roots. It was like I witnessed something spiritual, maybe some kind of Indian ceremony. I decided I would not talk about any of it outside the family unless I thought they might be able to shed some light on things. I knew I would have to find the right people if I was ever going to figure this one out.

Although I had many more unusual events in my life after November 2006, I want to stay on this one. I had a second experience with the lighted signs and symbols in November of 2010. Again, I was at the lake house, but this time with my son, Ryan. We had a deer drive the next morning. That night the lighted symbols returned, late. I awakened. No jab. No shadow people. Only lighted symbols. They flowed from the ceiling to the floor. This time I watched it for a long time. It went on for maybe ten minutes or so. Then it faded away. If I could have translated any of it, I had plenty of time to get part of the message. But I had no clue what it meant.

It would take many years before I would have a chance to understand more about those two nights. It was not until 2017, I was getting acupuncture treatments for my medical condition resulting from a car accident in 2011. My acupuncturist and friend, Maria Johnson, knew about my shadow people and the lighted symbols. I felt comfortable talking to her about them. She said she knew an Ojibwe medicine woman. She had told her about my 2006 and 2011 experiences. She thought we should talk.

Maria arranged for me to meet the medicine women at the clinic. I was looking forward to the opportunity for several reasons. One, because almost eleven years had passed with no answers. Two, I know about Ojibwe medicine men and women. They may have answers.

We met in 2017. She told me about herself, and I told her about myself. I shared that my mother is an Ojibwe Indian. I told her I met with spirit leader Fred Ackley, in 2007, and received my Ojibwe Indian name. She knew Fred Ackley well.

A medicine man (and woman) is a healer—a Midewiwin or Shaman—who relies heavily on Indian tradition with mystical elements going back to the original people. They have beliefs in the spirits, good and bad. They practice the art of healing through the use of herbal remedies, sacred items, and interaction with the spirit world. They are ceremonial people who take care of tribes. Their knowledge and skills are passed down within a family or a secret medicine society where their gifted privileges remain secret. The Ojibwe Indians do not talk about or promote their sacred practices. People outside the tribe are not permitted to know about the secret rituals or healing ceremonies. Indians believe the medicine men possess supernatural powers to cure disease and to control spirits. They believe they interact with the spirit world with the goal to bring spirits to the physical world for healing purposes.

I told the medicine woman about my experiences in Rice Lake. I told her about the shadow people dancing around my bed and the glowing symbols flowing down my dark walls. She intently listened to everything I had to say. She was so quiet I could not help but think maybe I sounded a little crazy. Maybe telling her was a mistake.

I felt like she would be polite to me. Maybe simply dismiss my unprovable event as a strange dream or nightmare. When I stopped talking, she closed her eyes for the ten longest seconds of my life. I was tired of having things happen to me that I could not prove. I did not know this person before this day. I had never heard of her before. As I waited for her to speak, I wondered why I did not just let the whole thing go. This was going to be my last time.

She opened her eyes. Her solemn face transformed. Her sharp eyes softened above a widening and gentle smile. Then she said I was spiritually reincarnated! She had worked with others who have experienced the exact same thing. The shadow people are spirits moving during a ceremony. The lighted symbols are known. The signs are Ojibwe! The assembly of the Ojibwe letters and words are prayers that are translatable. The symbols were presented in a spiritual medium—light and darkness. They flowed because the prayer was longer than what fit on the walls. She said I had witnessed my spiritual renewal, the rebirth of one of my souls!

I thought I had only one soul. The Indian nations believe we have three: an ego (mind) soul, a body soul, and a free soul. The ego soul is in the breath. The body soul provides energy to our body and life force for the awake state. The free soul is the soul that leaves the body during dreams. Because we believe I was awake for this experience, it means either my body or ego soul was going through a rebirth. At the time in 2006 and 2010, I felt I was awake, not dreaming. I had pinched myself to check. I had blinked my eyes several times. I am certain I was awake.

The Ojibwe believe the three souls communicate with each other. The free soul is the only soul that can leave the body in dreams and explore the dream realm. All three souls are equally important and powerful, and the dream world is as equally as important as the physical world. The mind and body souls do not dream. Anything that can happen in the dream world can have an impact (and consequences) in the physical world. It is in our dreams where the free soul gets spiritual guidance.

After meeting with the medicine woman, I kept saying to myself I witnessed a spirit ceremony. I was reincarnated. One of my souls was reborn, but why? Am I a new version of me? What does that even mean?

I believe this Ojibwe medicine woman is a gifted Indian. I also believe she told me truths that I needed to hear. After reading about the three souls and learning the importance of each, I am pretty sure we found each other in the physical world, in 2017, for a reason. The eleven years, between my first event and meeting a medicine woman, were filled with eagles, owls, Indian ceremonies, and dreams. But over that time, I had still not yet figured out what the shadow people and lighted signs meant. It was my 2017 meeting that put me on the course to learn more.

I found Ojibwe symbols like those on my walls. Even though I could not remember the order of the symbols to recreate the words and message, I did recognize the Ojibwe symbols. I found them in a book titled *The Book of Common Prayer**. It is for the administration of holy sacraments and other sacred rites and ceremonies translated into the Ojibwe Indian language. I do remember pyramid symbols and the letters X, C, P, and upside-down letters. There were others that flowed down my walls: dots and dashes in various configurations, pyramids on their sides, upside down, and incomplete with only two sides. I am now certain I saw prayers in the Ojibwe language. I know I witnessed an Ojibwe spiritual ceremony twice in my life. Maybe I will again. And maybe next time I will be able to translate some of the signs and symbols.

*The Church of Eagles' *Book of Common Prayer*, "Old Ojibwa Indian", written by Rev. J. Sanders.

24

 "Remember you belong to nature, not it to you."
—Grey Owl

November 2007—Ojibwe Indian Reservation

When I saw the great owl, I knew bad news would come my way. Seven days later they told me Uncle John Wayne died. I was saddened but not surprised. The great owl knew.

Although people attach a lot of different meanings to the appearance (and hooting) of the owl, most Native American Indian tribes view the bird as a harbinger of death. Some believe the bony circles around their eyes are made of the fingernails of ghosts. The Ojibwe Indians believe this ominous bird warns of evil and death and carries messages from beyond the grave. The Horned Owl and Screech Owl are the most feared—some say they are not real birds! The Cherokee Indians believe these owls are spiritual consultants for punishment and sickness. The Eastern Screech Owl is viewed by other tribes as medicine. And still there are some tribes that believe the owl was banished to nights as punishment for its lazy and annoying behavior.

The Bible sees the owl in very specific ways. The owl is symbolic for and connects to desolation and seclusion. They are a bearer of bad news for family and loved ones. Christian churches see owls as menacing and threatening symbols of evil. Many linked them to Satan. Because they are by nature silent and hide in the shadows of night, owls are seen as bad omens in most parts of the world. In all fairness, there are some cultures who see the owl as wisdom.

The Ojibwe Indians believe seeing (or hearing) an owl warns one of an impending death of a friend, relative, or well-known person. Because the owl is (generally) viewed as a symbol of change (most often bad), they appear in times of transition. For example, when relatives die it is a tragic transition. Also, the owl can appear before and around other kinds of change—divorce, breakups, and marriages. Seeing an owl in these types of transition means not to worry.

The Ojibwe also believe owls appear in dreams as symbols of wisdom or a warning. They believe when an owl flies over a person it is a simple message—the universe is watching over you. Life will be sorted out. No need to worry. However, if one hears an owl hooting in the night it is a bad omen. It brings death or bad news or bad weather. The direction the owl faces reveals point of origin, the place from where the bad news or bad weather emanates. If one hears an owl hooting in the night and the owl faces east, the bad news or death or bad weather is in the east and on its way to you.

I have had several experiences with owls, in my life. The experiences align with the long-held beliefs of the Ojibwe Indians (and other Indian nations). Although it is difficult for modern man to accept Indian myths, legends, and lore, it is equally hard for me to ignore it. Every time I encounter an owl, bad news follows. Some of my most significant owl experiences span a sixteen-year period. Each owl encounter preceded an unexpected death or bad news about a close friend or a family member. There have been too many events to ignore.

On November 20, 2004, I heard an owl hooting most of the night. It was unusual. I lived in my Minnetrista home, the one next to the sacred Sioux Indian burial grounds. It was the house where I would be visited by the white orb five months later. Prior to my November 2004 owl encounter, I had no owl encounters in Minnetrista. This night one hooted for hours—it clearly had something to say! I looked out each window but could not locate the owl in the trees around the house. Eventually the relentless hoots stopped, and I went to bed. Because I could not locate the owl, I assumed it was not here for me. Thus, bad news would not be coming my way.

The next day, I saw my neighbor outside. He asked if I had heard the owl the night before. I said I did but could not find it. My neighbor told me he had taken his dog for a walk last night and saw the biggest gray owl ever sitting on my roof. I cringed—the owl was here for me. Later, I got busy with work, organizing my annual poker tournament, and getting ready for the Thanksgiving holiday. I had all but forgotten about the gray owl. That weekend, my family left Minnetrista to visit grandparents and I stayed home to host thirty guys at the house for the poker tournament. The next morning—November 21, 2004—I got a call from dad. He was deer hunting in the Blue Hills east of Rice Lake. Five deer hunters were dead, murdered. The sixth, Dennis, my distant cousin, would die from his wounds the next day.

In February 2005, I had another owl encounter. It, too, was at my Minnetrista home. When I heard the hooting, it scared me. I thought, "What now, more bad news?" I had realized every time I heard an owl it signaled bad news for me. My father passed a few weeks later. He died in Jamacia on March 7, 2005.

By then, my business was taking most of my time and attention, and I stopped thinking about owls. I heard an owl hooting in June 2006, but I did not worry like I had before. I guess part of me wanted to believe not all owls are necessarily connected to something terrible. Then, on July 26, a few weeks after the owl hooted all night at Rice Lake, I got a phone call I did not expect. Grandma Kathleen, my angel, had passed. My rock was gone at the age of ninety-six. Was that what the owl was doing, easing me into knowing she was leaving this world?

Little time had passed after my 2004, 2005, and 2006 owl encounters, the deaths of eight—three family and five friends. In November 2007, I went on a deer drive with my distant cousin, David Drew. We joined eight other hunters in the Rice Lake area. After a good hunting day, he and I were leaving the woods looking forward to getting back home. On the way out of the woods, an owl, somewhere on the fringe, hooted so much that David and I could not ignore it. We started looking for it. I do not remember any other owl hooting as much as this one did that day. I did not want to say anything to David, but I was thinking the owl was really desperate to deliver bad news to someone. We found it on the edge of the woods in an old tree. I watched it pivot its head and its enormous eyes lock onto me. I think that owl stared at me for a solid minute before it blinked. It sent chills down my spine on that cold Thanksgiving Day. Five days later, my Uncle John Wayne, Neola's brother, died.

On December 31, I went ice fishing at Rice Lake with my brother Greg. Another big ole' owl hooted most of that New Year's Eve. I decided to go outside and look for it. I found it sitting in a nearby tree. This time, the owl did not look at me. It never turned. This time it kept looking west, locked on that direction. Since my family and friends were all east or south of Rice Lake, I was relieved. Maybe this owl was not sending bad news to me. But what was it doing, just hooting?

The next day—New Year's Day—I got an unexpected phone call from someone on the West Coast. They told me my good friend Roger had died. I had not talked to Roger for several years. After I returned to the Midwest, we lost touch. He was a good friend and associate with Conwood. Our lives kind of went in different directions. The sad news really broke my heart. Roger was a great guy. Then I realized Roger lived in Fresno, California. That city is west of me. The owl on New Year's Eve hooted up a storm with his eyes locked on the west. The loss of my friend was saddening but shocking as well. The owl did what they do. I could not stop thinking about all of my owl experiences since 2004. I prayed on New Year's Day not to see or hear another owl ever again!

I thought my prayers had been answered. I went a few years with no owls and no family or friend tragedies. I started to question whether the two were really connected. Maybe I was making too much out of the whole owl thing. Maybe it was just a series of coincidences. Owls are all over Wisconsin and the Midwest, and people die all the time. Maybe the owl thing is just one of those Indian myths shared around the campfire like stories of Bigfoot and other bizarre things in the woods. Maybe I had been overthinking the whole thing. Dealing with the eagles and orbs and shadows and scrolling symbols and signs had put me on overload.

The thing is, I continue to have owl and tragedy connected experiences on all sides of the family and my friends. It has gotten hard to ignore the Ojibwe Indian beliefs on owls. Although there is no scientific study I can point to, the bizarre powers of the owl cannot be easily denied. I think today I have more than enough actual experiences to say it is a real phenomenon. Yes, the Native American Indians believe the owl has these powers. They believe the owl has a specific role in the world. It may be a role modern science can never understand.

The death of Uncle John on November 27, 2007, would not only be a sad moment in my life, but it would also mark a

182

good time in my life. I was sad because I would not be with Uncle Wayne again. I was happy because I learned to look at death very differently. I attended my first Ojibwe death ceremony.

There was a man known by many as Grey Owl. He was a British-born conservationist that came to America and became a fur trapper and writer. He presented himself to others as a Native American Indian. Although he gained prominence as an author and lecturer, his true identity discovered after his death hurt his reputation for some. I mention Grey Owl because he loved the Native American Indians so much that this great man pretended to be one! I know he understood the world of the Native American Indian better than most. Grey Owl once said, "While scholars are comparing and contrasting theories, debating intellectual questions, and dividing humankind into categories, the world is changed by persons of faith, spirit, emotion, compassion, intuition, and irrational thinking." As I traveled to the Mole Lake Ojibwe reservation to attend Uncle John Wayne's funeral, I found words of people like Grey Owl captured my feelings, too.

My brother, Greg, and birth-mother, Neola, and I traveled to Uncle Wayne's funeral. We got to the Mole Lake reservation on day one of the death ceremony. To understand the Ojibwe beliefs about death you must first understand their beliefs about life.

They believe inside each of us is our Anishinaabe spirit. Our spirit inhabits our body during our lifetime, in this world. The Ojibwe Indian believes each of us is sent to this world by the Creator to accomplish something for the Creator. Once we successfully accomplish that mission, we can leave this world and go to a better place. It is the death of our human body and release of our spirit. Because we have pleased the Creator, death is a good thing!

The death ceremony is a four-day event. It is a combination of tribal celebrations, recognitions, prayers, and feasts around a special fire built on the first day. The tribal spiritual leader directs the death ceremony for three entities: the dead, the survivors, and the Creator. Fred Ackley, the spiritual leader for the Mole Lake tribe, has a very important responsibility. He must send spirits to the afterlife while protecting the living left behind. The spirits of the dead need four days to walk west to reach a place where souls dwell before they depart.

They say some souls linger. They may get lonely and try to take someone with them! The spiritual leader (Fred Ackley in our case) must guide the lingering spirits to the afterlife, as he protects the living. The Ojibwe Indians believe children are the most vulnerable. A charcoal smudge mark is put on the foreheads of the children. This protects them because when the spirits look at the child the face is blurred. It confuses the spirit and protects the child. Children are not allowed to attend a funeral. They are not allowed to make eye contact either. Normally the family of the deceased builds a fire in their home and maintains it four days. At the Mole Lake reservation there is a place for the death ceremony, fire, and gatherings. There are feasts. Meals are offered to the spirits in celebration. The Creator is pleased. The deceased has died the last time.

On the fifth day, the body of the dead is buried. Uncle Wayne's Indian name was Big Head. He was a big man; so big they had to build a larger coffin. I was touched by the ceremony for Uncle Wayne. I could feel the love and respect the Ojibwe people had for this good man. I will never forget the gray owl in the woods that told me his passing was near.

To my surprise, my great job filled my life in ways I would learn to appreciate years later. I knew Indians liked tobacco, but I did not know tobacco was way more than a plant grown for enjoyment. For the Native American Indians tobacco is a sacred medicine traditionally used in their rituals and ceremonies. I provided tobacco to many Indian reservations. The Ojibwe Indians believe tobacco is the first medicine gifted to them by the Creator. It is symbolic of respect, gratitude, and service.

During the death ceremony, following sacred food offerings, tobacco is used as a part of the ritual. Tobacco is offered to the Anishinaabe spirits. Tobacco is wrapped in a cotton cloth and offered to the spirits in one of three ways. It is placed onto sacred ground. It is placed onto sacred water. And it is placed into a sacred fire. There are prayers and chants before the tobacco is offered to the Anishinaabe spirits. During these prayers and chants the tobacco is always held in the left hand. It is because the left hand is the closest hand to the heart; this helps the flow of positive and kind thoughts. After the prayer, the tobacco is passed to the right hand, and then is placed onto the ceremonial grounds, water, or fire.

The Ojibwe Indians have four traditional sacred medicines. Tobacco is the first one. The other three are cedar, sage, and sweet grass. Birch bark is another important material. Chips of birch bark are placed inside the coffin. They are used by the spirit to build fires over the four-day journey. Sheets of birch bark are also used. It is wrapped around the body to protect it from harm during the journey.

The spirit travels to the land of the afterlife known as Minawaanigozigiwining or Gaagige. This is utopia—perfect happiness. The Ojibwe also place food and water into the coffin for the journey.

I learned more about the Ojibwe spirituality at Uncle Wayne's funeral. They see death as a good thing because the deceased completed their mission for the Creator and were now leaving this world for the last time, to utopia. The death ceremony is a time to think positive things about the dead, and it gives tribal members an opportunity to communicate with their Creator. In summary, the death ceremony is filled with prayer, song, chants, feasts, tobacco, and more. Even the drums have a purpose. They are used to help get the attention of the Creator. The death ceremony has been passed down over several hundreds of years.

I witnessed love, respect, and devotion for my Uncle Wayne. I was privileged to be a part of his incredible death ceremony. I was overwhelmed with the symbolism and rituals and how good I felt for my Uncle Wayne who we will miss but know he has accomplished what the Creator sent him to do. When I thought everything was over, the great Ojibwe spiritual leader—Fred Ackley—turned his attentions to me and my brother, Greg. I had no idea what was going to happen next. Stunned, in the moment, and honored to be in the presence of this great spiritual leader, I felt close to passing out. Somehow, I stood solid as the spiritual leader asked the entire tribe, approximately 100 natives, to join him in the next ceremony. Little did I know the next Ojibwe ceremony would change me forever.

25

"Be humble for you are made of earth. Be noble for you are made of stars." —A Serbian Proverb

November 2007—Ojibwe Indian Reservation

If you are unnamed, the Great Spirit will not know you when you try to pass into the next world. Anishinaabe means *original people*. It is the collective name of Indian tribes indigenous to the north American continent and includes the Ojibwe Indian nation. I did not realize most Anishinaabe communities (tribes) have a common origin and share traditions and values. The Mole Lake Ojibwe tribe has preserved (and practices) many of the Anishinaabe traditions still today. And that includes the naming ceremony.

My father, Dennis Roux (French and German), married

my birth mother, Neola Smith (Ojibwe), in 1961. I was born in September of that year, my brother in September of 1963. Because we have Ojibwe blood, we are eligible to receive an Ojibwe Indian name.

For me it began in 1992—my most memorable eagle encounter. Since then, I had more eagle encounters than I can count. That was when I began to study the Native American Indians and my Ojibwe roots. Then came the owls and the dreams and the visions. Then I would be visited by my father, in the form of a white orb! Then I would be visited by shadow people dancing in my bedroom, and the Ojibwe prayers on my walls. In November 2007, the owl visited and Uncle Wayne died a week later. Then I was at his death ceremony, overwhelmed. My knowledge of the Ojibwe ways helped get me to this point in my life. I fully embraced my Indian roots. At the close of Uncle Wayne's death ceremony, I was approached by the Mole Lake Ojibwe spiritual leader— Elder Fred Ackley. He told me he would lead the naming ceremony for me and my brother, Greg. We would receive our sacred Ojibwe Indian names!

The naming ceremony is a really big thing. In 1965, President Dwight Eisenhower visited the Ojibwe Indians. Later, they named the thirty-fourth president of the United States. They conducted a sacred naming ceremony and named him Giniw-Wi-Giizhig—the Golden Eagle. I later learned President Eisenhower had established the Indian Health Services for Native American Indians in 1954. This important development aimed needed medical resources and expertise to the Native American Indian communities for the first time. I can see why the spirits sent the name Golden Eagle to the spiritual leaders for this great president.

The nature of the Ojibwe people can be seen throughout history in their ceremonies and rituals and their ways. From the "War Path" to the "Marriage Ceremony" to the "Rituals of the Dead" and the dreams shared of eagles and spirits and the Great Creator, the Ojibwe people reveal their rich heritage and strong character. Noozwinkeng (naming) is another important cultural event. The naming ceremony is a ritual of enduring purpose. The process of naming is also one more way to preserve the attitudes and beliefs of the Ojibwe people.

In order for Greg and me to be named, spiritual leader Fred Ackley had to be asked by my mother or father (parent) before seeking a name for their children. The spiritual leader then seeks names through a spiritual process that can include fasting, meditation, dreaming, and prayer. Sometimes a name is given to the spiritual leader during the fast. Other times it can take many moons before the name is sent from the Great Spirit. All of this happens in advance of the planning of the naming ceremony. On this day, in November 2007, the spirits gave Fred Ackley our names.

Before I go there, I must explain. Like other Ojibwe ceremonies, tobacco is a part of the naming ceremony. The Ojibwe believe their prayers travel in the smoke that rises. The smoke delivers their prayers to the Great Spirit. Tobacco is one of many ways the Ojibwe Indians communicate with the Great Spirit. Tobacco is one of the most important spirit medicines. It is used often—before birth, during life, and after death. It is the first medicine given to the Ojibwe Indians and is used for sacred offerings often. How did I happen to work for a tobacco company?

The naming ceremony remembers the sacrifices of the Original Man who named everything before all men. During the ceremony and burning of tobacco, the spiritual leader announced Greg's name to each of the four directions that are the four cardinal points on the Ojibwe Medicine Wheel. They are represented with colors: yellow (east), red (south), black (west), and white (north). The four directions can also be interpreted as birth, youth, adult, and death. Or as seasons: spring, summer, fall, and winter. And as the elements of nature: fire, water, air, and earth. And as the four animals: eagle, bear, wolf, buffalo. And as the four ceremonial plants: tobacco, sweet grass, sage, and cedar.

At our naming ceremony, Fred Ackley announced Greg's Indian name to each of the four directions. After the spiritual leader called out the name, everyone present repeated Greg's Indian name—Giant Step. It is the Ojibwe belief the Spirit World then accepts Greg's name as Giant Step, and it is the first time they recognize the face of Giant Step. According to the Ojibwe beliefs, Greg is seen as a living thing for the first time regardless of his age.

Then Fred Ackley announced my Indian name to each of the four directions. And everyone present repeated my Indian name. I was in shock when I heard the name the spirits had given me. Suddenly, everything I had been through made perfect sense. There was a reason why the eagles kept coming to me. It was always bigger than I could imagine. The Spirit World told Fred Ackley my Indian name. How could this be? I could not have asked for any other name. Scott Roux's Ojibwe Indian name would always be White Thunderbird—Eagle! From that day forward we were guarded by the Spirit World and our ancestors. They would prepare a place for us when our lives here ended.

After the naming ceremony, I spoke to Fred Ackley. I thanked him for his special service for my family and Uncle Wayne, and for the naming ritual. I also asked about my father and my distant cousin, David. I asked why they went into those woods that day and survived the shootings. Fred Ackley said my father and David saw an eagle that morning. He said those who died or were injured did not see an eagle —they were not protected. Fred Ackley said my father and David were protected that day—the Great Spirits had other plans for them.

I have learned the Ojibwe ways. What touches my head and heart the most is how these humble American Indians live their lives today with such wisdom. I know they are more in touch with the real world than so-called modern man. I think we get lost in science and our cities of concrete, computers, and electronics. The modern man tends to overvalue our accomplishments and undervalue the wisdom of the cultures that came before, the cultures that embrace the vastness and the unknown. The culture that listens to the world around them. We are blind to all we cannot explain or understand when we should be in awe and recognize the secrets in life are too important to ignore.

My children would receive their Ojibwe Indian names.

My daughter, Kaitlyn, received the name Dancing Waters. It captures her joyful and energetic nature. My son, Ryan, received the name Spirit Moccasins. I am proud of this man. He serves our country. His Ojibwe Indian name captures his essence—Spirit Moccasins in the Ojibwe world means experience and vision. Over the last several years, Ryan has seen much. His experiences in the military will give him the patience and the vision to reach for the stars. I hope he continues to embrace the Ojibwe ways as he seeks value, purpose, and happiness in this life. The Ojibwe Prayer is something we can all live by to have a happy and full life.

Ojibwe Prayer:

Great Spirit, whose voice I hear in the winds and whose breath gives life to everyone, hear me. I come to you as one of your many children. I am weak and small and need your wisdom and your strength. Let me walk in beauty, and make my eyes ever behold the red and purple sunsets. Make my hands respect the things you have made. Make me wise, so I may understand what you have taught to my people and the lesson you have hidden in each leaf and each rock. I ask for the wisdom and strength, not to be superior to my brother, but be able to fight my greatest enemy, myself. Make me ever ready to come before you with clean hands and a straight eye. So as life fades away like a fading sunset, my spirit may come to you without shame.

26

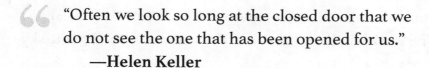 "Often we look so long at the closed door that we do not see the one that has been opened for us."
—**Helen Keller**

June 2011—Somewhere near Mankato, Minnesota

There is only one time in my life I thought I was dead. My wife got the dreaded call from the emergency room a little after 6:00 PM on a warm summer night—June 21, 2011. They said Scott had been in a car accident. He was in serious condition. She needed to get there as soon as she could—I'm sure my wife was more than worried. News like this devastates a family and can shake the spouse to the core. Add to it the burden of keeping emotions in check around the kids. No matter what you tell them they're going to think the worst, and they're going to think you are not telling them everything. Those innocent fears coupled with the unanswered questions make the whole thing a million times worse. Add all of that to the task of keeping a lid on your emotions during a long, tedious, heart-wrenching, three-hour drive to a hospital you've never heard of.

On the day of the accident, I was on my way from Mankato to a five-store chain in Sinclair. I was going to meet with management to restructure our contract.

I was on Highway 169 making good time, when I ran into major road work. I stopped to get directions, an alternative route to Sinclair. The best route was a dirt road through farmland. If it had rained that week, I would have gone a different way in my new company car—a 2011 Ford Escape. The week had been warm and dry without a cloud in the sky. I took the short cut.

In no time, I found myself in America's breadbasket surrounded by farmland. All around me, the crops were ready for harvest. I kept the car under 30 mph because there were other roads feeding or crossing my dirt road. I expected a tractor or combine to jump out in front of me at any moment. And to add to my problems, I was driving into a blinding sunset.

I approached yet another uncontrolled intersection, another dirt road crossing mine with no traffic lights or stop signs. I slowed down to twenty and eased into the intersection and got hit by a pickup truck! It shot into the intersection from my right. I had no time to react. The truck was speeding, going over seventy when it t-boned me on the passenger side. Every airbag in my car deployed as I was launched. I rolled into a field where my mangled, smoking car came to rest right-side-up. I was unconscious, pinned inside until the emergency crews arrived twenty minutes later and cut me out. In the ambulance, I heard them talking. The other guy was not injured. No tickets were issued even though the truck and Escape were totaled. They said it was an uncontrolled intersection and there were no speed limits posted.

At first, I thought I was lucky to be alive. I had survived a very dangerous wreck with what I thought were minor injuries. No open wounds. No blood. No terrible scars. I had a headache, neckache, and backache from all the airbags that saved my life, and from the jostling around as the car took the hit and rolled to a stop. The only thing broken was my right ankle. I think I can live with a foot cast for a few months. Lying on a gurney in the ER, I waited for my family and thought I would be fine after I got over my headache and the bumps and bruises.

My family finally arrived. After five hours in the emergency room, I was released. The ER doctor gave me pain medications. It was late on a Thursday night. He said to go home and convalesce over the weekend—icepacks on the aches and pains. I was to make an appointment to see my doctor on Monday to take a look at my broken ankle. I remember leaving the hospital that night with a limp and the help of my family. I remember feeling I really dodged a bullet.

We stayed in a hotel near the hospital that night. It was

late and no one looked forward to the three-hour ride home. We had all been through a lot. We checked into the hotel, and I hobbled into our room with a terrible headache. Everything hurt more. I took pain meds and headed for the bed.

I felt like I had been in a fight and lost every round. Why me? What does this all mean? Another pothole in life's highway. I helped my wife roll down the covers of our bed. We froze. My heart skipped a beat. The kids came over. We all stared at it. Sitting in the center of the bed was a quarter, eagle-side-up. Is it a message? I know everything happens for a reason. Then I immediately felt safe. I was being watched over. They found a way to let me know. I felt like everything was going to be okay. How else can I explain it. A bald eagle found its way to me, albeit a quarter eagle-side-up in a random hotel bed, on a random night, after a random car accident. The thing is, nothing is random in my life, everything has meaning.

The night in the hotel was unbearable. The three-hour trip home was unbearable. There were not near enough pain pills to help. The weekend in my own bed and on my sofa were awful. Something had changed. Everything got worse! My migraine headache was killing me. My neck, back, ankle, and every bone in my body screamed. My face changed. One side started to sag like I had no muscles in that part of my face. I lost control of one eye. It wandered. I started to stutter. I was forgetting simple things. I did not know if this was a normal thing after a wreck or if I was heading down a terrible road. The next day, I started to realize my injuries were not minor. I started to realize I may need some major medical help.

I went to a lot of doctors. I was diagnosed. I had suffered a traumatic brain injury. They call it a TBI. In the beginning, it affected my memory and speech. I would go through eighteen months of speech therapy. My memory loss would require a lot more. The doctors explained my sagging face. They call it drop face. It is also known as Bell's Palsy. It's a condition when part of the face droops due to swelling near a facial nerve. My swelling was due to the impact of the airbags on my face. This would take more than a year to resolve itself.

Wandering eye, known as amblyopia, is a result of my accident. My TBI led to a break between the brain and eye; they don't work together. This took a year to correct. But there were many more serious problems stemming from my TBI and nerve injuries. My severe migraine headaches continue today, more than a decade later. I have been diagnosed with RSD (Reflex Sympathetic Dystrophy or Complex Regional Pain Syndrome). It is a nervous system problem. I get a burning sensation in my limbs, feet, and hands for one. I have been diagnosed with CTE (Chronic Traumatic Encephalopathy). I suffer from moments of confusion, anger, sadness, and anxiety. I do not suffer with rage like often experienced by professional athletes suffering from this condition. I have been diagnosed with Cognitive Communication Disorder. It is a challenge to hold a train of thought.

I did not know June 21, 2011, would be the last day of my

life as I knew it. And I did not know that day would be my last day with my work. I would spend the rest of my life going to doctors and therapies to deal with my unending pain and inability to communicate and remember.

Because of the man I am, I have not lost faith. I firmly believe everything has meaning and everything happens for a reason. As I cope with my unexpected disabilities I search for the bigger meanings and my new purpose.

In my unshakable and very positive quest to understand my life, the good and the bad, I pray a lot. I am open with my feelings with my family and friends, and now my readers. I do not see any reason to hold everything deep inside. If I am sad, confused, or frustrated, I think it is okay to be out with it. My feelings are natural. They are there for different reasons. Letting them flow helps because I believe all the answers are out there. I cannot miss them by hiding.

I often talk to my daughter, Kaitlyn, about my car accident. She has seen me struggle through rehab and the major life changes. I asked her what she remembered most about that day. At the time, she was eight years old, in the third grade. Now, a college student at the University of Minnesota, she remembers she froze the second she was told her dad had been in a bad car accident. My family was directed to drop everything and get to a hospital (three hours away). Kaitlyn thought I was dead and that her mother was keeping it from her and Ryan for their own good. She thought her mother was simply waiting for the right time—doctors and hospitals do it all the time. Kids get no details. Kaitlyn also thought maybe I was not dead.

But maybe I was paralyzed or lost an arm or leg, or maybe I was blind or monstrously disfigured. She said the three-hour ride was the worst time of her life. She was in very dark places. Kaitlyn did say she felt off the whole day, way before she got the bad news. She said she felt a fight-or-flight feeling—desperation. It was a lot for a third grader to feel.

On a much lighter note, Kaitlyn remembered something special Ryan did that day. Her brother knew his little sister was struggling with the bad news about me. Usually, before going places in the car, the first one to call shotgun got the front seat. Not on that day. Ryan gave Kaitlyn the front seat. He climbed in the back alone. He knew she needed to be by Mom.

I did not die in my car accident on June 21, 2011. Later, after I got a look at the mangled Ford Escape. I knew I could have easily died on impact. A few seconds either way could have easily changed the outcome. But then I remembered what I learned at Uncle Wayne's death ceremony. The Ojibwe Indians believe each of us are sent to this world on a mission from the Great Creator. They believe we do not leave this world until we have completed our mission. If that is true, it is easy to understand why I did not die.

Did I live because my mission has not been completed? My Ojibwe name is White Thunderbird—Eagle! Is that just a random name the spiritual leader, Fred Ackley, pulled out of a hat? Or did he tell the truth? The spirits gave him that name for me. The quarter eagle-side-up on a random bed in a random room at a random hotel on a random night after a random accident on a random dirt road, was that whole thing random? Or did it all happen for a reason?

What do we really know about this world and this life? What is really happening here?

Am I overthinking when I search for meaning or am I on the right track? After a lot of thought, I believe the events that changed my life were not random. The accident happened to me for a much bigger reason than any of us could comprehend. Science cannot give us those answers. A statistician once calculated the chances of the random formation of DNA is equivalent to throwing a million marbles a million miles into the sky and they all return landing one upon another in a perfect, vertical straight line! So, DNA is not a random creation. Nothing in the universe is random. To think life is random is more bizarre than to believe in a God.

Can science explain miracles? No. They only have theories. Nothing can be completely proved. Then what? Science cannot explain tragedies either. And they certainly cannot predict outcomes from any tragedy. If they could, they would say Helen Keller suffered from an illness at age two and they would predict she would not live a normal life. They would be partially right. She lived a super-human life! Helen Keller lost her sight and hearing before age two. How is it possible she toured the world as an American author of fourteen books? How is it possible she became a world-renowned disability rights advocate and political activist and lecturer? How did a blind and deaf woman go to Harvard? How did she become known for her campaign for labor rights, women's suffrage, and world peace? This is only one example of the possible results after a so-called random tragedy.

I think everything is a purposeful gift from our Creator. Everything that happens in this world is not fully understood. I do not see how science will ever give me an adequate answer about why my tragedy happened, why I did not die, when will I heal, and what all of it will mean for me over the rest of my life.

At what point should we realize we need to look elsewhere for answers? At what point do we start believing the unbelievable? I think the Native American Indians are more in touch with the world around us than we—the modern world—will ever be. Somewhere along the way we have fooled ourselves into thinking we actually know a lot more than we do. Maybe that is not a good thing and there is a reason for it.

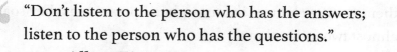

27

"Don't listen to the person who has the answers;
listen to the person who has the questions."
—Albert Einstein

October 2015—the woods of Rice Lake, Wisconsin

I always hoped for a special eagle experience for each of my children. I wanted them to feel at least one of the electric moments I have often. All things in nature are amazing, but for me there is nothing more moving than when a majestic eagle sees me, turns, and comes to me.

On a crisp October day in 2015, Ryan had an off-weekend from ice-hockey training. I planned to spend the whole day with my son. We decided we would go on a hike in the woods in Rice Lake. We got started at nine o'clock in the morning.

Ryan had a special goal. He wanted to find an eagle feather. I wanted him to have a moving eagle encounter.

An eagle feather is a symbol of honesty, wisdom, strength, courage, and bravery. The Native American Indians revere the bald eagle and golden eagle. They believe their feathers have great healing powers—both for physical and emotional injuries. Unlike other birds, this raptor (bird of prey) has a wingspan up to ten feet. An eagle can climb to 10,000 feet (5,280 feet is a mile). Fortunately, most planes fly five-to-seven miles up. Eagles can soar for hours; because they have thousands of very light, yet very strong, feathers arranged in efficient layers. These feathers also protect the bird from weather—insulate from cold and rain—and help them endure changes in atmospheric pressure as they soar almost two miles above.

The Ojibwe Indians have used eagle feathers in rituals and ceremonies for thousands of years. Some Indians hunted eagles. They are also believed to be among the first domesticated animal. The Indians used eagle meat for spiritual feasts. Each time they killed an eagle they prayed during every step in the process of preparation and the feast. Eating eagle meat ended long ago because most indigenous Indians believed it was a spirit bird—a messenger between man and the spirit world. Eagles were then only killed for their feathers, feet, and bones, items used in clothing and jewelry, headdresses, prayer sticks, and other religious articles.

It is believed walking on the path to a fallen eagle feather is a sacred event. A message is sent. Guidance to step back from a certain situation in life. Guidance to give yourself more time to make an important decision. Coming upon an eagle feather is believed to be a sacred gift from the spirits. It means they are watching over you. You are not alone in deciding something of importance or in planning your future. Because the eagle is such a powerful spirit animal, their feathers also symbolize the act of rising above a challenge and never giving up. The Ojibwe say the one who finds an eagle feather will feel the message immediately—it is said to be the first thought one has after they see the eagle feather for the first time.

Ryan, Kaitlyn, and I have often talked about the Ojibwe beliefs. They are aware of their Ojibwe roots and my special relationship with eagles. I love that they both embrace the world of the Ojibwe Indian nation. It is an important part of their lives. Parents always hope for the best for their children. We look for signs that tell us where they are in life and how they are doing. My heart was touched when I heard what Kaitlyn said at the end of an interview related to the creation of this book. She said, "Now, whenever I'm with my dad, I see eagles almost every time. It's like they take turns keeping an eye on him." I am so pleased she sees it. She believes.

On the perfect day in October, Ryan and I set out to find an eagle feather. Ryan describes an eagle feather as something like a cross or rosary. It has religious meaning. And he sees it as a good luck charm, a way to stay close to our Creator—God. We hiked for nine hours. We went deep into the woods. We walked up and down hills, spurs, and draws looking for an eagle feather. Ryan was determined. He thought if we could find an eagle nest maybe somewhere on the ground below would be a feather.

The sunset was around 5:40 PM that day. Dusk crawled into the woods as the big ball of fire continued to sink deeper beneath the horizon. All day we did not see eagles or find a feather. Then it happened! Ryan said it was the biggest eagle he ever saw. It came out of nowhere! It flew right over our heads just above the trees. We stopped and watched the awesome bird glide with effortless grace. I watched my son take in another cherished moment.

When it passed over our heads, we turned and followed it. There it was! An eagle feather perched on a low hanging branch. The feather was inches from Ryan's eyes. Seconds before he bent down and passed under the limb. I thought it was significant that we both missed it on our own. When the eagle appeared, we stopped in our tracks. The eagle's flight path made us turn around and look back. Its path guided Ryan's eyes to the feather enveloped in the tiny twigs and brittle leaves of the low hanging branch he went under. I wonder how many eagle feathers we missed that day. I wonder if the eagle came to help us.

To this day, we are amazed to find an eagle feather perched at Ryan's eye-level. While containing our excitement over the feather, we continued to watch the majestic bird as it looked back at us until it disappeared into the forest. We said a prayer as we stared at the eagle feather nestled in the hand of a giant elm. It was as if that tree would not allow the feather to touch ground.

We wanted the eagle feather, but there are rules. Laws. It

is illegal to possess an eagle feather. Even one you find in the woods. The eagle, and all its parts, are protected by federal law. Only certain people are allowed to possess an eagle feather, and even they must obtain a federal permit each time. If someone finds an eagle feather in the woods, regardless of good intentions they cannot take it without a valid permit. The penalty is a fine of up to $2,500 and one year in prison for a first offense. Ignorance of the law is not a defense. No slaps on the wrist.

For thousands of years, the Native American Indians used eagle feathers for religious and cultural purposes—healing, death ceremonies, marriage, and name ceremonies. Due to the urbanization of America and rampant poaching, the eagle became endangered. In 1940, the federal government passed the Bald Eagle Protection Act to protect the bird. Out of respect for the rituals and religious needs of the American Indian, the National Eagle Repository was established. It provided dead eagles to them. This repository is the only place where dead eagles go. Every aspect of each eagle received is recorded: cause of death, condition of feathers, age, species, what is missing, and more. If any part of the eagle is missing, it is noted and investigated. If the cause of death is suspicious, it too is investigated. Wrongdoers are prosecuted to the full extent of the law.

The only people to possess eagle parts, and who qualify for a federal permit are those members of a federally recognized Indian tribe. Once a permit is given, the recipient can only get one dead eagle from the federal repository at a time. It can take up to three years to get a second dead eagle.

Today, there are more than 4,000 people waiting for their one dead eagle. The Federal Repository gets 900 dead eagles each year. Once a tribe receives a dead eagle (in a frozen state), they are responsible to track every part of that eagle—the feathers, claws, bones, etc. If a federal agency asks where parts are, the tribe must be able to track every single part of their eagle. If they cannot, they are prosecuted—fined.

It is illegal for anyone to sell, purchase, barter, or trade genuine eagle parts. The feather can only be passed to direct members of a family over generations, and only for religious purposes. Under no circumstance can an eagle feather be given by a Native American Indian to a non-Indian. The rules are strict for a reason. There was a time when the eagle was an endangered species.

As Ryan and I looked at the pristine eagle feather stuck between the twig-fingers of a branch, we could only take pictures and say a prayer. Although we are members of the Ojibwe Indian nation recognized by the federal government, we did not have a permit. Even if we did have a permit, we would not be authorized to take an eagle feather from the woods. Even a Mole Lake Ojibwe tribal leader is not authorized to take an eagle feather from the woods. If a dead eagle is found, it must be frozen and sent to the federal repository. An investigation follows. Killing an eagle is a federal offense punishable by prison time and major fines.

When I think how important the eagle has been and is today to the Native American Indians, and how important the eagle is to the United States Federal Government, it really strengthens my beliefs in my spirit animal. I look back to the day in 1992 when I first encountered an eagle, and the day in 2007 when I was given my Ojibwe name. Both events changed my life forever. I know the sacred Ojibwe naming ceremony happens after the prayers of the medicine man—spiritual leader Fred Ackley—are answered. The spirit world decides. They chose my name. I will be forever honored, humbled, and vigilant. Everything matters.

28

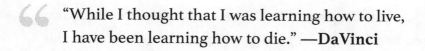

> "While I thought that I was learning how to live, I have been learning how to die." —**DaVinci**

Grandma Kathleen often said to me, believing in something greater than ourselves gives us a chance to be more. The Native American Indians have great stories, sacred rituals, and lessons of life they have passed down for generations over thousands of years. Their primary teachings are embodied in the Circle of Life, also known as the Medicine Wheel. I have taken the time to study them. In concert with what Grandma Kathleen taught me, I found them to be helpful in my quest to understand my life journey.

I believe everyone needs to find something they can believe in whether they are religious or not. The Circle of Life teachings could be the answer you have searched for.

The Ojibwe Indians shared beliefs have withstood the test of time, unchanged! That fact means a lot to me. They are sound. And I believe they help answer the three most important questions we all have: who am I, why am I here, and what is life all about?

The Ojibwe Indians believe all things are connected and life is a continuous process. We move in what they call a Circle of Life. It reveals and symbolizes the natural cycle of birth, growth, death, and regeneration for all living things. Because I have been involved with the Mole Lake Ojibwe Indians a good portion of my life, I have taken the time to look at these teachings. They have had a major impact on my life.

As the story goes, life is like a rose. The Creator took a seed and planted it in Mother Earth. The winds tilled the soil, and the rains watered the sprout that grew stronger every day. First came the thorns to protect the fragile new life in a challenging world. Then came the leaves to catch the Sun and the water to feed the plant that would grow bigger and stronger. Then came the bud, and only then could the beautiful rose follow. The rose depended upon many things; the seed from the creator, the wind, the rain, and the Sun. The thorns had to be successful protecting the plant from the dangers in the world. The rose depended on thorns as much as the seed and the Sun and the wind and the water. Then, the rose dies one day. The plant decays and falls back into Mother Earth. But then a new seed. And then it all comes back. And this time it also needs the gifts of life. And then it lives again and dies again and decays again over and over and over.

The Ojibwe Indians see all life like the rose! We each are born, we each learn, we each face dangers, we each have needs and have gifts. And then we flourish. But the day comes when we will die, and decay and we will be reborn. Will we be a rose? Will we be stronger and wiser? Or will we be something else? The Ojibwe Indians believe there is a time in the life circle for birth, growth, reflection, meditation, awareness, acceptance, to surrender, and rebirth. The rose is eternal life. Each of us are too, and so is everything in the world. The Native American Indians believe life is an everlasting process. They speak of this process as the circle of life. They associate every stage of our evolution with a place on the medicine wheel.

We are born and move through a childhood phase where certain things are experienced and certain lessons are learned. We then move into the youth phase where more experiences of discovery and existence in the world occurs. In this phase, new lessons are to be learned before we go to the next point on the circle of life. We eventually move into the adult-parent phase. Again, because of what came before we are ready for what comes next. The adult phase is one of responsibility and contribution. Then we eventually move to what they call the elder-death phase. The American Indians see death as just one more point of transition of a continuous life. We reach the death phase only when we have accomplished our unique mission that had been given to each of us by the Great Creator. The Indians view death as a reward. It is a good thing. It is a time of celebration. It is a time when our spirit can now be set free from the body that was given us for this world. Our death is when we meet the Great Creator's expectations. Our reward is to move to a place where we make the next decisions. Do we choose to enter the glorious realms of the everlasting light? Or do we choose to return to this world, but with greater wisdom and knowledge and gifts? Because we achieved our mission, we are rewarded with such decisions by our Great Creator. This I believe is the only difference between living things. However, we may choose to return as a spirit animal or bird or creature.

The Circle of Life is described as having four primary directions and four spiritual gatekeepers—the East, South, West, and North. Just as the Sun circles the earth we move on the Circle of Life in a clockwise direction. Each point on the circle has a season, element, animal, plant, color, and heavenly body. Each direction exposes us to certain/specific life lessons, and we gain certain/specific knowledge and qualities of existence. These teachings are eye-opening. I saw how my life connects with the Circle of Life. I could see my life movement around the circle, and for the first time in my life, I could understand where I am and where I am going.

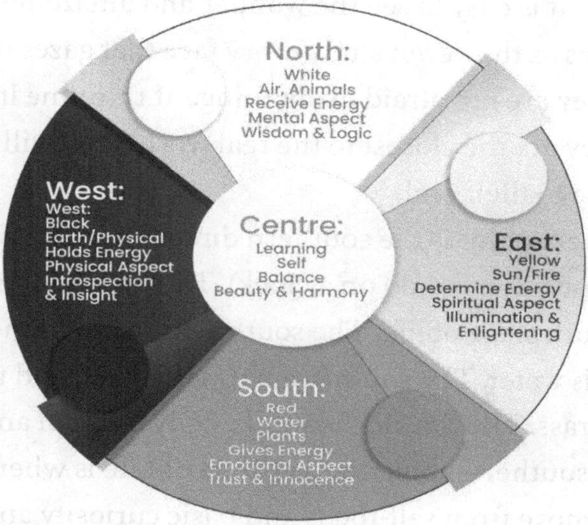

The eastern direction of the Circle of Life (the position is 3:00 on a clock). It is where the Sun rises in the morning and brings wonderful light and warmth and new knowledge. It is the birth and child stage of life. It is also described as a specific season—spring—the time when new life appears and begins to cover the earth. The east element is fire. The east animal is an eagle. The east plant is tobacco. The East's heavenly body is the Sun. The East's color is yellow, and the eastern direction on the Circle of Life is where we first learn to interact with the world. It is the time when we have the greatest opportunity to learn how to communicate with everything that walks, swims, crawls, and flies. We can truly communicate with the trees and rocks and everything else in nature because all things in nature move on the Circle of Life. If you have ever watched a baby, you will see they study everything—a cricket, a star, a tree, a leaf, a ball, a dog, a frog, and more. It is easy to see the wonder and amazement in a baby's eyes as they even study every face that gazes upon them. They are not afraid of anything. At this time in the circle, they are the closest to the real world they will ever be until close to their end.

The next point is the southern direction in the Circle of Life (the position is 6:00 on a clock). The South is described as the youth stage of life. The south season is summer, and element is water. The south animal is the wolf, and the plant is sweetgrass. The South's heavenly body is Earth and color is red. The southern point on the Circle of Life is where we begin to move from self-focus and basic curiosity and wonder to a state of more community awareness. It is in the South that we begin to see we are part of something much bigger than ourselves. It is a time in growth when we begin to understand how to work (and be) together as opposed to work (and be) alone. The South is where we prepare to leave behind our self-focused ways.

Prior to my eagle encounter in 1992, my life focus was mostly self-oriented. Even though I always valued the family connection, my life in the military and later in California focused on my own goals of accomplishment, education, and career. All of which related completely to my own priorities and life. After I learned about the Ojibwe Indian's Circle of Life it became very clear to me when I moved from self-focus to more. I think I can pinpoint when I moved from the south point on the Circle to advance the greater good.

The next point is the western direction on the Circle of Life (the position is 9:00 on a clock). I know my eagle encounter in 1992 marked my movement from the South to the West. After my eagle encounter, I felt a new and strong urge to return home. Something pulled me back to my homeland two years after my eagle encounter. I would return to the place where I was born and was a boy living with trust and innocence. The Midwest is where my family and friends and my early memories stay. Two years after my eagle encounter, I left California ready for something else in life. I had changed. My self-focus melted away. Now it was all about family, community, and roots. In three more years, I married. Then, a few years later, I started a family. The western point on the Circle of Life is my time for nurtured harmony, balance. It is my time in life to flourish.

The northern point on the Circle of Life (the position of 12:00 on a clock) is the phase after the West. It is the time of wisdom and the time of preparations for death. It is the time we each leave this world. When we each enter the North, we can see the gates to the realms of eternal light. Before we see these gates, we live and think often about our death. We grasp our limits in this form. Prior to the North we did not give our death much thought. Older people often say the young people think they are going to live forever. While in the North we think in terms of how long we have left. We ask ourselves what have we done? We review our mistakes and successes. And we advise the West, the South, and the East. But they do not listen. They are not ready to hear the truths of the North.

The northern point on the Circle of Life is where we overcome the weaknesses that held us back in the East, the

South, and the West. For the first time we understand the most damaging weaknesses are ignorance and fear. In the North, we gain a new clarity of thought. The things we did not understand over our lives become very clear. In the North, we embrace our failures and simply set them aside. They are a part of our journey no more. Whatever held us back in life is no longer important or relevant. In the North, we are victorious over the weaker emotions that haunted us in the East, South, and West—the most useless emotions of shame and guilt. In the North, we only think about the entirety of our human journey. We think about our mortality, and we mentally prepare for our next transition we call death. The Ojibwe Indians believe it is in the North that we prepare for our death. Sometimes we know and other times we may not know. But we all feel our greatest and ultimate decision of this life. Do we choose to enter the eternal light, or do we choose to return to this world with greater wisdom? They say this decision is made when we close our eyes for the last time in this life.

29

> "Grandfather, sacred one, teach us to love, compassion, and honor, that we may heal the earth and heal each other." —**Ojibwe Prayer**

As I became more involved in studying my Ojibwe roots, I soon realized the words Grandma Kathleen shared when I was a child were probably the most important words of all. As I grew up in the eastern and southern points on the Circle of Life, I must have been so self-focused I missed a lot. But Grandma Kathleen never stopped saying it. She understood where I was in my development. She was at the North. She had the wisdom. She understood what was important. And she was giving back to those behind her on the Circle of Life. She often said these words. She said, "When we believe in something greater than ourselves, we have a chance to be more."

Grandma Kathleen's words first touched me as I entered the western phase of my world on the Circle of Life. I had entered a time of introspection. I wanted to know more about life and how I fit in. Grandma's words came alive when I studied the Ojibwe ways. That is when I found the Seven Grandfathers and the set of Anishinaabe guiding principles that work for everyone.

The foundational (or traditional) story that gives rise to the teachings of the Circle of Life are the teachings of the Seven Grandfathers. It is their guiding principles that have been passed down for many generations and serve as the guide to living a good life, one without conflict, one with peace and harmony in this world.

It is said early in the history of mankind the creator spirits—known as the seven grandfathers—had the responsibility to watch over the Anishinaabe people. It is said they sent a Messenger Spirit to earth to communicate and teach their values. The Messenger Spirit was asked to first evaluate the human condition. The Messenger Spirit found it to be not good. Then the Messenger Spirit came upon a baby. The Seven Grandfathers approved the Messenger Spirit to take the baby around the world for seven years to learn the Anishinaabe ways of life. Then the Grandfathers took the baby, now a young boy, for another seven years. They taught him love, respect, bravery, truth, honesty, humility, and wisdom. As I studied these seven principles of the Ojibwe Indian nation, I saw they were similar to the Christian's Ten Commandments. I was raised in the Catholic Church. I had been exposed to these teachings throughout my life.

Out of curiosity, I looked at other historical belief systems in the world like the Ten Commandments. I was surprised to see how similar these laws are to those of the Seven Grandfathers. In Judaism, there are the seven laws of Noah. Although these laws are worded differently, they too are similar. The Seven Laws of Noahide are traditional, too, but presented in a different way. Instead of saying, love Mother Earth, it says do not worship idols. Instead of saying, love and respect, it says, do not curse God. Do not commit murder and do not commit adultery. Like the teachings of the Seven Grandfathers, the Laws of Noahide say the same thing but in an opposite way. Do not to steal. Do not to eat the flesh from a living animal and establish courts of justice.

The Anishinaabe teachings deal with truth and humility and respect of others and the earth and love and honesty and bravery and wisdom in a positive way. I personally like the way they are shared with mankind. I believe the teachings of the Seven Grandfathers are some of the most commonly shared teachings in the world. Even if someone is not a native Indian, they can adopt these beautiful teachings. They are for anyone who wishes to honor others and desires to live a full life.

Because these teachings are truly good and can benefit everyone, I wanted to understand them fully. To break these teachings down more, it was important to learn that the Ojibwe Indians begin with what they call the first rule. If we do not take care of Aki (Mother Earth) we will not have a home. I think it is very telling that this is the first rule. The Native American Indians live close with Aki. They believe it is our responsibility to make sure everything the Creator gave Aki is always there for the next generations. There will always be debate on this topic. Many believe we are living on this planet with borrowed time. Even though I do not believe that, I do think we all should do what we can to conserve energy and protect this planet.

The Ojibwe teach—every day we should greet those who came before us. They are referring to all those who came before us whose spirits are still in this world. They believe those who chose to return to this place with more wisdom and in any shape they wished, those are the spirits in all the miracles. They are everywhere that we can see and smell and touch. The Ojibwe awake each day and speak to the many generations of spirits that came before them.

The Ojibwe Indians also see the young people straying from the sound principles that promise a full life. They see them not giving thanks to all this world has given them. But it is the responsibility of the elders in this world to participate in raising the awareness of the younger generations. The ways of Mother Earth and the community of life can then thrive.

As we all try to understand who we are, why we are here, and what life is all about, I find the teachings of the Seven Grandfathers, which connects with other teachings in the world over thousands of years, must hold the keys. So, I took each teaching apart. I boiled it down to its most basic meaning and could see why it is so important to me in my life, and everyone else.

Grandfather Debwewin is all about truth. He says truth allows us to believe in a greater power than ourselves. Like Grandma Kathleen said, it allows me to be a more complete person. Truth also allows the youth to see, even though their journey seems slow, it encourages them to keep moving toward their destiny.

Grandfather Zoongidiewin is about courage and bravery. These keys allow us to make positive choices and face our inner fears. Courage allows us to have conviction based on our good decisions in life that may not be popular but are right. This allows us to live free for our betterment and the betterment of family and community.

Grandfather Manaajiidiwin teaches us respect. When we learn and practice respect, we can best live in a community because we treat others as we wish to be treated. When we have mastered respect, we cannot harm others. This is another foundational teaching we must adopt.

Grandfather Gwayakwaadiziwin teaches us integrity. Why is this one of the most important tenants of life? Because it teaches us to focus on knowing and accepting who we are. It reminds us we are very special, and we benefit in no way by trying to be something we are not. It is through integrity that we are given the ability to survive and thrive in this world.

Grandfather Zaagiidiwin teaches love. This is represented by the eagle. It is in the core of all teachings. It is the most important. It gives us balance, peace, and allows us to graciously accept all things given us by the Creator.

Grandfather Nibwaakaawin teaches wisdom. It is only with wisdom that we can use our inherent gifts wisely. It allows us to see the differences between us and others in a respectful way. It matures our ability to listen with a sound mind. Wisdom is vital to understanding who we are and why we are here. We must listen.

Grandfather Dabasendizowin teaches humility. This helps you answer the question of what life is all about. Humility allows us to see we are a sacred part of all creation. It allows us to have pride and to praise our accomplishments. Humility helps us find balance between ourself and the miracle of all creation of which we are a part.

The Seven Grandfathers' Instructions for My Life

- Nibwaakaawin taught the child—to cherish knowledge is to know wisdom.
- For me: childhood, high school, military, college, career, and Ojibwe research.
- Zaagidwin taught the child—to know love is to know peace.
- For me: birth at Deaconess, Grandma Kathleen, Packers game with dad, and the orb.
- Manaadjitowaawin taught the child—to honor all creation is to have respect.
- For me: Grand Canyon with Kaitlyn, Indian mounds, Ryan's feather, Ojibwe mother earth.

- Aakodewin taught the child—bravery is to face the foe with integrity.
- For me: my dad's Carnegie hero award, deer drive shootings, PTSD with my dad, my disabilities, my life in Nevada.
- Gwekowaadiziwin taught the child—honesty in facing a situation to be brave.
- For me: learning challenges, deer stand murders, my automobile accident and recovery.
- Dibaadendizowin taught the child—humility is to know you're a sacred part of creation.
- For me: Ojibwe eagle encounter, Rice Lake eagles, dad's funeral, the owls, Ojibwe teachings.
- Debwewin taught the child—truth is to know all of these things.
- For me: career choices, tobacco, eagles, orbs, mounds, Indian ceremonies, the Circle of Life.

When my life began at Deaconess Hospital, I did not know my path. Today, it is clear to me I have been in good hands. When I felt below average, scared, alone, and lost, I was moving in the Circle of Life. The spirits were watching over me. They brought to me the lessons and the experiences I needed to grow and to overcome my inadequacies and weaknesses. The spirits moved me forward in life. They never abandoned me. They held me up until I could stand on my own, until I understood. Every experience in this book is a part of me. I moved in the East and the South of the Circle of Life. Then my eagle came in '92. From that day on

they watched over me. Then I moved to the West in the
Circle. I took a hold of my life. I listened to the sacred
teachings of the Ojibwe Indians and the Catholic Church.
My great spirit is the Father, the Son, and the Holy Ghost. I
made a bold decision to return to my homeland. It led to
marriage and a family. Then I bonded with my father and my
Ojibwe roots. That was when I knew everything has
meaning. I knew the time would come when I understood.

30

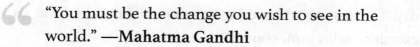

"You must be the change you wish to see in the world." —**Mahatma Gandhi**

I was told, in 2014, I was done. I thought my injuries would eventually heal. What had started as a terrible migraine, a sore back, and a broken foot turned into so much more. This is the rest of the story.

After my car accident, on June 21, 2011, I found the eagle-quarter in my hotel bed eagle-side-up! I was optimistic. I had the faith. Eagles have always been good for me. Everything was going to be okay. Later, the doctors, my therapy program, and encouragement helped me cope with the daily disappointments. I knew it would be a long battle, but deep down I felt like I was losing ground. No matter how hard I worked, I continued to slip deeper into the dark abyss. Days turned into months and months turned into years. I did everything I was told but I still got worse. After three long years of small successes and continued decline, the doctors could no longer look at my condition as temporary. The day came in 2014. My doctors broke my heart.

2014—Rice Lake

My pain management neurologist did not mince words. He said I would never work again—I was done! In desperation, I told him he did not understand. I needed to work, or I would wither away and die. He said the most I could ever hope for in the future was part-time jobs and maybe volunteer work. I would be limited to just a few days a week and a few hours a day. The tasks would need to be minimal. But wait, I was an executive sales professional!

I could not remember much after the wreck. My short-term memory went fast. Someone could tell me to go outside to get a newspaper. I would go outside but have no idea why I was standing there. To add to my short-term memory problems, I started to lose life memories. I knew family and friends, but I could not remember some past experiences. First, I lost pieces, and then I lost all. Some memories would return only to disappear again.

I could not hold a train of thought. I would wander all over the place and forget what I was talking about. For a long time, I did not even know I was doing it. When I got to the place where I knew, I still could not stop bouncing around. Before my accident, I was an accomplished executive sales representative always performing in the top 5 percent of the company. I was a very successful businessman with a college degree. To be an accomplished sales professional, one must be highly organized and have exceptional communication skills. I did. And my life was always busy. I traveled 70 percent of the time. When I got home, I would be involved in numerous activities (sports) with the kids and family. I was an avid sportsman, baseball player, hunter, fisher, and hiker. I went to church every Sunday, did volunteer work, and spent time with the Mole Lake Ojibwe Indians. I was financially strong, owned two homes, took vacations. After my accident and three years rehabilitation therapy, my comprehension dropped to a third-grade level. I could not communicate like before. And I was in constant pain. The accident stole my career and everything I had worked for all my life. Then the accident took my family!

They told me the airbags saved my life. I will agree they kept me alive, but they did not save my life. They, in fact, played a major role in destroying my life.

The laws of physics cannot be changed by an airbag. An object in motion stays in motion unless acted upon by a counter motion. My human body inside my car was in motion. I was going north until my human body was forced to go east by a two-ton truck traveling 70 mph. The airbags popped out instantly during that major change in my motion. Airbags placed enormous forces on my human body! Every cell and every organ and every bone in my body was traumatized by immense forces even though I was inside a so-called balloon cocoon of protection. The airbags could not change the basic laws of physics. The intensity of the

counter-forces that altered my human body's motion
damaged cells, tissues, organs, and bones. In my case, the
greatest damage was to my brain and spinal column.

My primary injury is RSD—Reflex Sympathetic
Dystrophy. It is regional pain syndrome due to a damaged
nervous system and immune system. It is a condition where
the nerves do not communicate with the brain properly.
Signals in the body are not always sent to the brain correctly.
In doctor terminology, my neurological impulses do not flow,
they explode and scatter messages and confuse the brain. For
example, phantom pain is pain experienced when there is
nothing wrong. It still hurts! Imagine how it would feel to hold
your hand in boiling water. If you suffer from RSD, you feel
the exact pain, but your hand is not in boiling water. The brain
gets bogus signals. You suffer just like when it is real. Your
only option is to be medicated, and that numbs your whole
body. Some medicines to manage RSD put you in a medicated
stupor while you try to get to the next day. You wake up to new
pain experiences. Maybe your hand is not in boiling water, but
your leg could feel like it is on fire. Your hand could ache. Your
skin on your foot could turn purple and swell up.

I must learn to live with my nervous system problems in
addition to mental disabilities from my brain injury. I wake
up each day with new problems. My RSD can deliver more
severe pain, or unbearable spasms and cramps, or stiffness
and swelling. I may have extra sensitivity to hot and cold, or
lose my hearing, or even lose my sight. I may have
discoloration of skin, or loss of muscle control, or I could

wake up with half my body paralyzed. Each time I do not know if it is temporary or permanent. That fear alone is hard to live with.

My world turned upside down in 2014. At the age of fifty-four, I would never work again! I would be disabled the rest of my life. I would live in a constant state of discomfort with restricted mobility and a different set of problems each day from my RSD menu of nightmares. My car accident caused all my injuries, and my injuries caused the changes in my life.

The terrible news—I would never work again—pulled my eyes out of the sky and forced me to take a closer look at me, my life, my marriage, and my future. I was forced to look at all the things we either take for granted, overlooked, rationalized, or set aside because we were too busy or didn't want to rock the boat.

In 2015, my life changed course again. One year after I was told I would never work again, my son has a major opportunity. Ryan had a chance to advance in his sport—ice hockey. He had a chance to get on a path to a professional career. My son was invited to play on a high- level hockey team—a tier-one level. As a high school senior, he had a window of opportunity in a very competitive market. To pursue his dream, he would have to leave his home in Wisconsin and live in Texas. Ryan was too young to live alone, and I was in no condition to go with him—my pain was too great, my rehab too intensive, and my mobility too limited. After a lot of discussion, we all decided his mother would go with him to Texas. Little did I know the separation would open eyes for all of us.

It would be a turning point in my marriage. We had been struggling for years but we were too involved in other things to deal with it head-on. Although we tried to fix what was broken, we eventually reached a point of no return. After twenty years of marriage, we decided to go our separate ways. The divorce was final in October, 2017, exactly twenty years to the day that we got married. Although the kids were almost grown up, close to being on their own, I agreed to take full custody. They would be leaving the nest in no time.

We three—Ryan, Kaitlyn, and me—continued to live at our home in Rice Lake. The once happy place on Minnow Lake changed. Divorce hurts everyone. In a short time, my son joined the Army and went overseas—Italy. My daughter decided she wanted to go to college at UMD—the University of Minnesota in Duluth. Even though her decision would leave me alone in Rice Lake, I would not stand in her way. It had to be her decision. I would support her.

Not too long after the divorce, I found myself alone in the woods in Rice Lake. It had become a lonely, depressing place. It was my rehab center on Minnow Lake away from the world. I was alone, disabled, and suffering from RSD. I was medicated and surrounded by emptiness. I knew I could not live my life like that. It was not who I was, or who I wanted to be—a man limited in life by his injuries. I had lived a life with many challenges and rebirths. Everyone knows Scott Roux never gives up. Things needed to change.

The doctors said I would not get better. They also said I

could better adapt to RSD if I lived in a mild climate. Wisconsin and the Midwest, the place where I grew up, was too harsh. The place I had come back to after the Navy, college, and my career, was now the place I needed to leave. The accident on that dirt road forced me to leave my homeland. That accident would be what made me change my life yet again.

I did my research. Where could I go that would meet my new needs? Where would I want to live the rest of my life? It had to be in the sunbelt—a more temperate climate. I looked at Florida and Arizona, the first two places that came to mind. I added San Diego to the list, fond memories in my Navy days. There was a place in Oregon I liked, but I quickly decided against it because it was a difficult place to get to. One of my priorities was a hub, so I could travel back home when I needed, and Kaitlyn and Ryan could visit. I eliminated California because of the cost of living. People are leaving that state en masse.

I had to settle on a place that not only had a temperate climate but also a low humidity, a reasonable cost of living, an airport hub, and a place that felt right for me—hard to explain that one. I decided Florida was too humid. I crossed it off my list. San Diego is beautiful but like all of California it is too expensive. I liked a lot of the benefits of Arizona, but in the end, it is still a desert—flat, sand, cactus, rattlesnakes, and horny toads. And I need hills and trees and grass. In no time, I had crossed everything off my list and started to get nervous. Was I going to find a place in America that would work for me? Then, a very close friend of mine had a suggestion. Anita mentioned Boulder City, Nevada!

I had honestly never heard of Boulder City, and never even considered Nevada. I took a look, did my research and discovered it met all my criteria: no state income tax and reasonable cost of living, temperate climate, trees and hills (and mountains), a hub nearby—easy access for the kids and my travel back home. The major airport was twenty miles from Boulder City, the McCarran International Airport in the Las Vegas Valley. Boulder City is seven miles from the Hoover Dam and a few hours from Eagle Point at the magnificent Grand Canyon. I visited Boulder City and found it even met my last requirement—it was a place that felt right for me. I could see myself living there, and that was important.

In no time, I sold the Rice Lake property and loaded up the moving truck. What happened next blew me away. I had not been thinking about my eagles for quite a while. My thoughts were other places—my declining condition, my divorce, my kids leaving the nest, and my desperation to find a place where I could start the next chapter of my life. I pulled out of my driveway at Rice Lake and one last time looked back at the house my father built. The place where we had so many years of happy family times together. The last place my father lived before he left this world after the Deer Stand Murders. The place where eagles dropped feathers on our dock and filled the trees and grounds around us on occasion. I turned to the road ahead and pressed the pedal to the metal—time to roll. Then it happened!

The beautiful, majestic, awesome eagle came at me. She hovered just above the road in front of me. She wanted me to see her. She turned and I turned several times onto different roads. She led the way. It was as if I was being escorted out of Rice Lake. This giant eagle stayed with me, and one sat in the same tree, on the same branch, like the day of my father's funeral—never before or after. The eagle led the way to Highway 48 and stayed with me another mile. I knew then it was not over for me. I knew then there were going to be more great things in my life, and there were going to be more eagles. They would find me in Nevada. Then I realized, out of all the places I could have gone, I had picked the one place in the temperate climate areas where eagles live! Was it in the back of my mind all the time? The last thing on my list was that I had to feel right about the place. Boulder City, Nevada, felt right. And my new home happens to be just right for my spirit animal, the eagle!

31

"The future belongs to those who believe in the beauty of their dreams." —Eleanor Roosevelt

October 2021—Boulder City, Nevada

I moved to Boulder City in 2020, into my single-level townhouse—1,400 square feet with two bedrooms and a view of Lake Mead out my living room windows. I was ready to open the next chapter of my life. I was not going to roll over and die! I will not let RSD take everything from me. My plan is to take baby steps forward. Try to improve a little each day. I will be positive in all that I do and I will never, never, never give up.

In the beginning, Kaitlyn did not like the idea that her dad would be so far away—Minnesota to Nevada. I had always been close, all of her life, even her college life. I think

Kaitlyn liked knowing her dad was only a few hours away. We talked often. I wanted her comfortable with my move. I was still only a few hours away, by airplane. I know she will never be 100 percent okay with it, but she knows it's important to me.

On the other side of the emotional coin, Ryan is okay with wherever I choose to live on the planet Earth. He is an independent man currently based in Italy. The world has already gotten a lot smaller for him! I think there are many benefits of military life. And that is one. I remember after I crossed the equator a few times with the Navy the world shrunk for me, too.

The doctors did not take everything from me. I may never work again, but I can be a volunteer a few days a week. It is important to me to stay busy. If not, I know I would just wither away. I cannot sit at home and look out the window and watch the world go by. I cannot feel sorry for myself.

The way I see it, RSD gave me a new career. I am no longer in the sales business. Now, I am in the service industry. My new job is to help people in need. It is my reason to get up in the morning. When I am not doing volunteer work, I am preparing for it, or I am in rehab or enjoying my life. I have a routine. I have responsibilities. I no longer allow RSD to be the focus of my life.

I did volunteer work in the past, prior to Boulder City. We brought up our children by involving them in volunteer work at the church and in the community. We taught them early the importance of giving their time and services to those less fortunate. The way I look at my new life is very important. I see volunteer work as my new career, in retirement. Doing volunteer work makes me feel alive. I feel I am doing something important. My paydays are those special times when a child from a broken home smiles even just a little. Or when the old man in the wheelchair shakes my hand. I feel I am doing exactly what I should. I am exactly where I am supposed to be. We all fight change because we fear the unknown, or because we don't have control. Because I believe everything happens for a reason, I can handle life's changes a little better. I must admit I still have heart palpitations sometimes. I am only human.

I started with what I like to call an introductory agenda. I eased into my new duties. Back in 2017, I did volunteer work at the Rice Lake Senior Center. I served food and beverages to the elderly. I did anything I could to make them comfortable. Later in Rice Lake, I took part in the Kinship Program. I started in the fundraising area. Then I became a mentor for a young fellow with a troubled family life. I enjoyed helping him. We had regular work projects together. I did my best to teach him things to help him in life. We went fishing and hunting together, and I took him on boat rides where we talked about life. I did my best to help him on his journey.

In Rice Lake, prior to 2020, I participated in volunteer programs with the Knights of Columbus. I helped sell tickets to KOC events. I served meals, and I had assigned prayer duties. My time to be at the church praying for others was from midnight to two o'clock in the morning. I had a list of names, people struggling in life. I also prayed for me in those wee hours. I always asked God for guidance. In those late hours alone with God, I got ideas and courage that would take me from the security of my home in Rice Lake. I realized I was a retired, single man with disabilities. It was time for me to start a new chapter of my life story.

When I moved to Boulder City in 2020, I did not waste time. I looked for volunteer work. Like what began at Rice Lake, I knew I needed to continue my volunteer work. But now it would be a central part of my life. The key to my happiness for me is to stay busy and not focus on problems all the time. I really wanted to help people. I had that light burning very bright in my heart all my life.

In Boulder City, I learned about the St. Jude's Ranch for Children. They are dedicated to helping children who have been abused, including teenage girls rescued from sex trafficking. I felt so good about my mentoring work in Rice Lake that I believed with all my heart I could help some of these children rebuild a life of trust and happiness if they let me.

The interview process was long and involved. St. Jude's took their time looking me over. They investigated my background with a fine-toothed comb. It did not offend me in the least. I understood their need to know everything about the people they bring into their program. They are dedicated to protecting their children from all forms of danger, including a volunteer with less than honorable intentions or one lacking the skills they need. I am sure some of the children are so fragile they cannot handle even one more traumatic experience in their young life. St. Jude's wants to be certain people around these kids have a positive impact.

While I waited for the St. Jude's opportunity to develop one way or another, I started my volunteer work in Boulder City at the state-sponsored senior center. There I served food and refreshments to residents. Because I had not heard back from St. Jude's for so long, I had assumed I was not qualified. Maybe my disabilities were too much to handle. But then, when I least expected it, I got the call. I was cleared. I had survived their intensive investigation. My disabilities were not a problem. St. Jude's offered me a volunteer position and I took it.

I cannot express how important the St Jude's volunteer work is to me. I am a part of the team that takes care of the foundation that helps children with little broken hearts. Although I do not work directly with the children, I view all my assignments and responsibilities as important. I support the great work of the professional staff with the same commitment I have to serve the senior center. At St. Jude's, I help by doing anything I am asked from cleaning the church and helping in the gift shop and mailroom. I have learned to accept my limits and to not allow them to stand in my way. I hope one day I will be given more responsibilities.

My new career in Boulder City has come together as planned. I have important responsibilities. I provide services to people in need at both ends of the Circle of Life. I have a place to be. I have people who need me.

How much more could I ask for? I love life and continue to be amazed by my journey. The miracles of life continue to flow in spite of all our efforts. Although my physical challenges continue take a toll, I live in the environment (climate) that gives me more control over RSD.

I believe having my days laid out is important. I have a primary responsibility to report to work at St. Jude's and the senior center as scheduled. I must be prepared to give my best. My other responsibility includes daily productive rehabilitation therapy. I force myself to do those things that will help advance my level of comprehension. My reading level is still not where it needs to be but is steadily improving. My goal is to return to my college level. I know I will get there one day.

I also continue to focus on my God and my Ojibwe roots. I believe the teachings of the Circle of Life are compatible with my Christian beliefs. As I move in the Circle, I trust each stage I leave and enter. I am in good hands. There is always a place on the Circle for you and me. The important things I have learned are: I am never alone and all the important things in life are there for all of us. For me, my eagles remind me of these truths all the time.

EPILOGUE

" "My life is my message." —Richard De Vos

October 2021—Boulder City, Nevada

It is my hope that my journey provides surprise triggers for those seeking their own answers. When you turn the pages, I recommend the three guiding principles that opened my eyes, my heart, and my mind to my journey.

These guiding principles helped me navigate some of the most bizarre experiences that turned out to be pivotal in my life. Trusting our judgment over others give us the strength to see what has been hidden. The answers we seek are in the places we have not looked.

- My first guiding principle is: nothing in life is random.
- My second guiding principle is: everything has meaning.
- And my third guiding principle is: we know very little.

Don't let what you think you know hold you back. I hope you enjoy my journey and benefit from my discoveries. It is my sincere wish that you find the answers to the greatest mysteries of your life. And remember one thing. In times of confusion and doubt listen to your heart.

I had good times and bad. I have been blessed and cursed. I have climbed life's mountains and fallen into the dark abyss. I have witnessed the unknown and unexplainable, and I have done the impossible. I have learned much.

Here are Scott Roux's five secrets to life:

On the day of my birth, I was given last rites. Clearly, the most educated people in these medical things thought I was going to die. And clearly, they were wrong!

MY FIRST SECRET TO LIFE IS: be open to the unknown. We cannot explain far more than we think we can explain. Don't fall captive to the arrogance of mankind. The experts do not have a door into the unknown. They are limited by partial knowledge, theories, tools, skepticism, and speculations. The miracle of life and the endless universe are far too complex for us to ever comprehend fully. I learned not to dismiss the unknown. I learned man does not have all the answers. Embrace the miracle of life. Do not let others limit your miracles.

My SECOND SECRET TO LIFE IS: there are angels among us, find one and stay close. After my near-death birth and my parents' divorce, I felt alone and confused. But at the age of five, I was placed in the arms of an angel—Grandma Kathleen. Anyone who knew her knew she was an angel! Even our Catholic priest. Grandma Kathleen had time for me when I was most fragile. My father was at work all the time and I did not have a mother in my life. I was teased at school —Scott doesn't have a mother. Grandma Kathleen was always there for me. She helped me with my confusion and delicate feelings. Grandma Kathleen taught me to pray—she gave me someone to talk to any time I wanted or needed. She invested a part of her life in me. She made me feel okay. There are angels in the world. If you are hurting or confused, I recommend you find one. You just have to look for an angel. I promise you will find one.

GRANDMA KATHLEEN GAVE ME MY THIRD SECRET TO LIFE— believe in something bigger than you. She didn't give it a name. And it does not require a religion. Everything we want or need is in this world. We just need to search for it and commit to it. The Christians have God. The Ojibwe Indians have the Great Spirit. Others have Allah or Buddha or Brahma or Ganesa or a spirit animal or a place on Earth like Eden, or the Sun or Jupiter. Your God is gracious, merciful, all-knowing, holy, all-powerful, a grantor, and a protector. It is important to believe in something bigger than ourselves, so we can become bigger than we are. Your God is where you go for refuge, help, understanding, guidance, and answers. I cannot put enough weight on this secret to a good life. The day I found my God, I found a place to go and someone to talk to about anything and everything. Once I found my God, I was never alone again.

MY FOURTH SECRET TO LIFE IS: pray with all your heart and soul and often. When we talk to our God the right way, we get answers to all our questions. People say they do not hear from God. I say it is probably because you are not listening. You may still be detached, not fully committed. You may want answers your way, on your timeline. I did not get answers until after I learned how to have a relationship with my God. My prayers suddenly turned into conversations. Always begin with giving thanks for all of your blessings, the things you take for granted, but if you lost just one of them your life would change drastically: your health, family, a roof over your head, your job, food, clothing, and those gifts that make you special. We all have gifts. Only after giving true thanks are you ready to ask. When you are aware of your many gifts, you will hear answers to your questions. I make prayer a part of my day. I call it my alone time. And I can promise you things happen when you ask the right way. It's magical.

MY FIFTH SECRET TO LIFE IS—everything has meaning. Like the title of this book this secret is probably the hardest to accept. The day I trusted everything happens for a reason, I started to see my path in life. Things do not happen for no

reason. I am who I am and where I am as a result of everything in my life. My birth and last rites, the son of an Ojibwe Indian, the grandson of Grandma Kathleen, the son of Dennis Roux, my struggles in school, my job at the machine shop, my stint in the Army and Navy, my college life in California, my career, my eagle in 1992, my return to my homeland, my marriage, my children, my eagle encounters, the Deer Stand Murders, Uncle Wayne's death, my Ojibwe naming ceremony, my father's death, the sizzling orb, the Indian mounds, the owls, the shadows and writing on my bedroom wall, my car accident, the owls, my divorce, my volunteer work, my RSD, my move to Boulder City, and my work at St. Jude's. Every one of those define me. Everything has meaning. The sooner we embrace this the sooner we are unafraid of life! Our eyes are open to revel in the miracles of our world. It is wonderful to know I am a result of so many wonderful people and incredible events in my life, and God values me like every star in the universe and grain of sand on every beach. We are each a part of the enormous miracle we call life.

Grandma Kathleen and Grandpa Larry

Dennis and Francine Roux

Greg Roux, Scott Roux and Jeff Crisp

Ryan Roux

Kaitlyn Roux

John Wayne Smith

Neola Smith

Chief Willard Ackley and Og-go-ma-qua,
my great, great grandmother
(She lived to age 125.)

Everyone has a heart.
Use it in a good way.
If anyone has a broken heart or bad heart or
unknown heart, empty heart or twisted heart,
we good hearts must help the weaker hearts or the
hearts that need us,
and make them good hearts.
It will be a better world if we all have good hearts.
—Scott Roux

ACKNOWLEDGMENTS

I want to thank Steve Bradshaw for his patience and understanding with me while writing this book. Steve is an amazing writer. I could not have done this without you.

I also thank Anita P. for her support and follow through. You helped me find the words.

I also appreciate my publisher and the staff at Zamiz Press for their belief in me through the last leg of this process.

And I give a special thank you to the Drew family for their support of my dad and I during the deer hunter tragedy.

ABOUT THE AUTHOR

Scott Roux is passionate about life and sharing what he's learned with others. Scott feels that all people have potential. He's made it his goal to help the next generation find their purpose.

When he's not helping people, he can be found around family and friends.

You can connect with Scott at his website: www.Author-Scott-Roux.yolasite.com

CPSIA information can be obtained
at www.ICGtesting.com
Printed in the USA
JSHW030802260922
30847JS00001B/6